SKETCHES

OF

American Policy.

Under the following Heads:

I. Theory of Government.

II. Governments on the Eaſtern Continent.

III. American States; or the principles of the American Conſtitutions contraſted with thoſe of European States.

IV. Plan of Policy for improving the Advantages and perpetuating the Union of the American States.

By NOAH WEBSTER, Jun'r. Eſq.

With a new introduction by

John R. Vile

Professor and Chair,
Political Science Department,
Middle Tennessee State University,
Murfreesboro, TN

THE LAWBOOK EXCHANGE, LTD.
Clark, New Jersey

ISBN 978-1-58477-856-1

Lawbook Exchange edition 2008, 2025

The quality of this reprint is equivalent to the quality of the original work.

THE LAWBOOK EXCHANGE, LTD.
33 Terminal Avenue
Clark, New Jersey 07066-1321

Please see our website for a selection of our other publications and fine facsimile reprints of classic works of legal history:
www.lawbookexchange.com

Library of Congress Cataloging-in-Publication Data

Webster, Noah, 1758-1843.
Sketches of American policy under the following heads : I. Theory of government, II. Governments on the eastern continent, III. American states, or, the principles of the American constitutions contrasted with those of European states, IV. Plan of policy for improving the advantages and perpetuating the union of the American states / by Noah Webster ; with a new introduction by John R. Vile
p. cm.
Reprint. Originally published: Hartford : Printed by Hudson and Goodwin, 1785. With new introd.
ISBN-13: 978-1-58477-856-1 (cloth : alk. paper)
ISBN-10: 1-58477-856-3 (cloth : alk. paper)
1. United States--Politics and government--1783-1789. 2. Federal government--United States. I. Title.
JK155.W38 2007
320.973--dc22

2007031077

Printed in the United States of America on acid-free paper

Noah Webster: Proposing and Promoting Stronger National Union Through the Power of the English Language

Noah Webster was born in West Hartford, Connecticut, on October 16, 1758. He was a distant cousin of Massachusetts Senator Daniel Webster.[1] Noah earned an undergraduate degree (and later a Master's degree) at Yale, taught school for a time in Goshen, New York, and studied law at Litchfield, Connecticut. He began his law practice at a time when he was becoming engrossed in writing, most of which was directed to school students.

Before long, Webster's life in letters overtook his career in law, to which he would later return and again abandon. By 1785, the year he published his *Sketches of American Policy*, Webster had already published his 3-volume *A Grammatical Institute of the English Language*, which included a speller (often called the *Blue-Back Speller*), a grammar, and what a biographer has described as "the first literary anthology for children ever published and . . . the first . . . containing a significant amount and variety of literature by American authors."[2]

By the end of his life, Webster had become known as America's greatest lexicographer, but in 1785 he was still a young man who authored his *Sketches* for the purpose of convincing

---

1. Daniel Webster (1772-1852) used orations to unite the nation, much as Noah used his books for the same purpose. For an excellent biography, see Robert V. Remini, *Daniel Webster: The Man and His Time* (New York: W.W. Norton & Company, 1997).

2. Harlow Giles Unger, *Noah Webster: The Life and Times of an American Patriot* (New York: John Wiley & Sons, 1988), p. 80.

the public of the need to strengthen the Congress under the Articles of Confederation. At the time of the Constitutional Convention of 1787, Webster was living in Philadelphia. He was chiefly concerned with getting authority for Congress to protect copyrights (he had already succeeded with getting individual legislation within some of the states), which he recognized was essential to his future livelihood.[3]

I

Webster's *Sketches*, and the Constitutional Convention of 1787 can best be understood in their historical context, which they in turn help to illuminate. In 1776, representatives of 13 former colonies in North America declared their independence from Great Britain. Within days, they further explained their reasons by adopting the stirring words, initially penned by Thomas Jefferson, proclaiming that "all men are created equal" and possessed "unalienable" rights of "life, liberty, and the pursuit of happiness." The Continental Congress that adopted this Declaration of Independence and commissioned George Washington as commander-in-chief of American forces found it more difficult to draw up a plan of government to replace British rule. Proposed in 1777, the last state (Maryland, a small landlocked state, which had held out until larger states gave up their western land claims) finally ratified the Articles of Confederation in 1781.

---

3. Irah Donner, "The Copyright Clause of the U.S. Constitution: Why Did the Framers Include It with Unanimous approval?" *American Journal of Legal History* 36 (July, 1992), 361, 370-72. A record of Webster's reflections on his efforts respecting copyright laws are found in Noah Webster, *Collection of Papers on Political, Literary and Moral Subjects*. New York: Burt Franklin, 1968. Originally published in New York, 1843, pp. 173-78.

The Articles were best typified by Article II, which provided that "Each state retains its sovereignty, freedom, and independence, and every Power, Jurisdiction and right, which is not by this confederation expressly delegated to the United States, in Congress assembled."[4] The unicameral Congress that the Articles created was relatively weak. Although states could send more than one representative, each state had a single vote. Congress had no power over interstate commerce, and it could request, but not compel, states to furnish taxes and militia forces. The Articles required the consent of nine states on most matters, and required unanimous state consent to ratify amendments.

In time, leading statesmen recognized that the centrifugal forces within the Articles were too strong. America could not raise adequate funds to pay its debts and fulfill other financial commitments, and contemporaries questioned whether it could adequately protect states against domestic insurrections. American diplomats found that foreign governments did not treat the United States as an equal on the world stage. American leaders further worried about the nation's ability to defend itself.[5] Some Americans were also troubled about abuses of human rights that were taking place within states, where legislatures usually dominated and governors were generally quite weak.[6]

---

4. See "Articles of Confederation," in Winton U. Solberg, *The Federal Convention and the Formation of the Union of American States* (Indianapolis: The Bobbs-Merrill Company, Inc., 1958), p. 42.

5. See especially, Max M. Edling, *A Revolution in Favor of Government: Origins of the U.S. Constitution and the Making of the American State* (New York: Oxford University Press, 2003). Also see David C. Hendrickson, *The Lost World of the American Founding* (Lawrence, KS: University Press of Kansas, 2003).

6. One of the best portrayals of this time period, which focuses on conditions at both the state and national levels, remains Gordon Wood, *The Creation of the American Republic, 1776-1787*. Chapel Hill: University of North Carolina Press, 1969.

Introduction

Leading statesmen like George Washington, Alexander Hamilton, Gouverneur Morris, and James Madison, Jr., recognized that a stronger government was needed. The wooden amending process served on several occasions to block reform of the existing document, but leaders pressed ahead. After delegates from Virginia and Maryland held a successful meeting at Mt. Vernon in March 1785 to discuss common problems of navigation and commerce, they called for a convention of all the states to meet at Annapolis to engage in similar conversations. Although only five states sent delegates to this Annapolis Convention, which met in September, 1786, it in turn became the springboard for expanding the agenda and calling what became the Constitutional Convention of 1787. In part frightened by the outbreak of Shay's Rebellion in Massachusetts in the winter of 1786 – a rebellion that had so disturbed Noah Webster that he published a letter directed at the malcontents that was called "The Devil is in You"[7] – 12 states (all but Rhode Island) eventually decided to send delegates to Philadelphia. A total of 55 delegates attended and hammered out a Constitution that continues, in amended form, to this day. As in the Confederation Congress, each state had a single vote at the Convention.

The Annapolis Convention had called the Philadelphia Convention "to take into consideration the situation of the United States, to devise such further provisions as shall appear to them necessary to render the constitution of the Federal Government adequate to the exigencies of the Union," and to report this plan back to Congress and to the states for their unanimous recommendation.[8] Delegates from Virginia exceeded this charge by boldly introducing a plan (the Randolph or Virginia Plan, of

---

7. See Unger, *Noah Webster*, p. 118.

8. From Resolution of September 14, 1786 as found in Solberg, ed. *The Federal Convention and the Formation of the Union of the American States*, pp. 58-59. The term "Foederal" is the original spelling.

which James Madison was probably the primary author), in the opening days of the Convention that essentially proposed an entirely new form of government. It proposed substituting what we today call a federal government for a confederal system (although the details and terminology of the new arrangement still needed working out); a bicameral for a unicameral Congress; three branches of government –legislative, executive, and judicial– for the single legislative branch; representation based on population rather than state equality; and numerous other innovations, many of which became the subject of subsequent compromise.

Even the New Jersey Plan, which William Paterson proposed as an alternative to the Virginia Plan after about two weeks of debate at the Convention to retain equal representation for the states, embodied many of the innovations, including a bicameral legislature and separation of powers, that the Virginia Plan had introduced. Although the Convention eventually proceeded with the Virginia Plan, delegates introduced numerous emendations and compromises, the most famous of which – the Great, or Connecticut, Compromise – provided for representation according to population in the House of Representatives and equal state representation in the Senate.

II.

Given its age, its historical influence, and its ongoing importance, historians and political scientists continue to seek to understand the origins, the theories, and the controversies that are embodied in, and that surrounded, the document. The chief sources in this endeavor have been some of the historical documents noted above, the Notes of the Convention, especially those of James Madison (who conscientiously assumed an unofficial role as secretary),[9] *The Federalist*,[10] debates from state ratifying conventions, and other contemporary writings for and against the document.

Such interest is not new. In 1804, 17 years after the Convention, Noah Webster wrote a letter to James Madison upon the death of Alexander Hamilton asking Madison's opinion on a eulogist's claim that Hamilton had been the first to run for Congress with the idea of "establishing an efficient general government." Webster suggested that Madison might himself have been the first to push for a new plan of union through a resolution in the Virginia legislature, but Webster observed that he had published his own "Sketches of American Policy" in 1785 and had carried a copy to George Washington prior to the Convention. Webster commented:

> The remarks in the first three sketches are general, and some of them I now believe to be too visionary for practice; but the fourth sketch was intended expressly to urge, by all possible arguments, the necessity of a radical alteration in our system of general government, and an outline is there suggested.[11]

---

9. Max Farrand has collected Madison's notes, those of other delegates, and relevant correspondence in *The Records of the Federal Convention*, 4 vols. (New Haven, CT: Yale University Press, 1937; paperback edition, 1966). James H. Hutson subsequently published the *Supplement to Max Farrand's The Records of the Federal Convention of 1787* (New Haven: Yale University Press, 1987). For a recent abridgement of Madison's notes, see Edward J. Larson and Michael P. Winship, *The Constitutional Convention: A Narrative History from the Notes of James Madison* (New York: Modern Library, 2005).

10. Originally published in a New York newspaper, these 85 essays were penned by Alexander Hamilton, James Madison, and John Jay under the pen name "Publius." They have been published in numerous editions. As important as the essays are, readers need to understand that they were works of advocacy, designed to support adoption of the Constitution.

11. "Letter from N. Webster to Mr. Madison," "New Haven, August 20, 1804." In Noah Webster, *Collection of Papers on Political, Literary and Moral*

He added, almost by way of apology, "As a private man, young and unknown, I could do but little, but that little I did."

Canvassing his memory as well as he could, Madison, who continues to be called *The* Founder,[12] but who just as consistently denied being the solitary "writer" of the Constitution,[13] arguably downplayed Webster's role while still sharing credit not only with Hamilton and Webster, but with others as well:

> The change in our government like most other important improvements ought to be ascribed rather to a series of causes than to any particular and sudden one, and to the participation of many, rather than to the efforts of a single agent. It is certain that the general idea of revising and enlarging the scope of the federal authority, so as to answer the necessary purposes of the Union, grew up in many minds, and by natural degrees,

---

Subjects. 1968 reprint of 1843, p. 168. Citing a letter from Noah Webster to James Kent of October *20*, 1804, at the Library of Congress, Harry R. Warfel, *"Introduction" to Sketches of American Policy* (New York: Scholars' Facsimiles & Reprints, 1937), p. i, similarly observed that Webster had presented his *Sketches* to George Washington in May, 1785 and to James Madison in November, 1785 and that "Mr. Madison expressed himself pleased with the pamphlet," which Webster then proceeded to tie to a resolution Madison introduced in the Virginia House of Delegates to call the Annapolis Convention.

12. See, for example, Marvin Meyers, ed. *The Mind of the Founder: Sources of the Political Thought of James Madison* (Indianapolis, IN: Bobbs-Merrill, 1973).

13. Robert A. Rutland records that in responding to a letter in 1834 whose author called Madison "the writer of the Constitution of the U.S." Madison modestly observed that "You give me a credit to which I have made no claim." Madison further observed that the Constitution "was not, like the fabled Goddess of Wisdom, the offspring of a single brain. It ought to be regarded as the work of many heads & many hands." See "The Virginia Plan of 1787: James Madison's Outline of a Model Constitution," *This Constitution* no. 4 (Fall, 1984): p. 23.

> during the experienced inefficiency of the old confederation. The discernment of Gen. Hamilton must have rendered him an early patron of the idea. That the Public attention was called to it by yourself at an early period is well known.[14]

In the preface that he composed sometime between 1830 and 1836 for the posthumous publication of his records of the Federal Convention, Madison further observed that "A resort to a General Convention to remodel the Confederacy, was not a new idea." He observed that Pelatiah Webster, Noah's cousin, had published a pamphlet in 1781 recommending the necessity of calling a convention "for the express purpose of ascertaining, defining, enlarging, and limiting, the duties & powers of their Constitution."[15] He noted that "In 1785, Noah Webster whose pol. & other valuable writings had made him known to the public, in one of his publications of American policy brought

---

14. "Reply to the foregoing," "Hon. Jas. Madison, Washington, October 12, 1804," *Ibid.*, p. 170.
15. "James Madison's Preface to Debates in the Convention," in John R. Vile, *The Constitutional Convention of 1787: A Comprehensive Encyclopedia of America's Founding*, 2 vols. (Santa Barbara, CA: ABC-CLIO, 2005), II, 886. Hannis Taylor wrote a pamphlet in 1912, now generally discredited, claiming that Pelatiah Webster was the chief author of the Constitution. See Hannis Taylor, *The Real Authorship of the Constitution of the United States Explained: James Madison and Pelatiah Webster Defended by Hannis Taylor Against Attack* (Washington: U.S. Government Printing Office, 1912). Pelatiah Webster's central contribution to the drive for a new constitution appears to have been his suggestion that if the states retained all their powers, the confederation would be "a union without bands of union, like a cask without hoops." Unger, *Noah Webster*, p. 84, claims that this analogy "became the watch cry of every political speech, every newspaper article, and every dinner toast by those who sought a new constitution."
16. "James Madison's Preface," II, 886.

into view the same resort for supplying the defects of the Fedl. System."[16]

Webster wrote his *Sketches of American Policy* between February 16 and 25 of 1785 and published them in Hartford on March 9 of the same year.[17] In the advertisement that precedes and accompanies his own first essay, Webster himself referred to the appearance of "Dr. Price's pamphlet." Richard Price, an English dissenting clergyman who had favored the American Revolution and to whom Congress had extended citizenship, had published his own "Observations on the Importance of the American Revolution; and the Means of Making it a Benefit to the World" in 1784. Like Webster, Price had advocated vesting greater powers in Congress, the disestablishment of religion, and opposition to the slave trade.[18]

III.

Webster's *Sketches of American Policy* appear to have been widely known by the delegates, many of whom he had visited on tours through the states promoting his books. Webster had

---

17. See Warfel, "Introduction," to *Sketches of American Policy*, p. i., citing Emily E.F. Ford and Emily E.F. Skeel, *Notes on the Life of Noah Webster* ([Privately printed]: New York, 1912), I, 125-26.

18. See "Price, Richard," in Vile, *The Constitutional Convention of 1787*, II, 623. Also see Carl B. Cone, "Richard Price and the Constitution of the United States," *American Historical Review* 53 (July, 1948): 726-47.

19. Drawing from Webster's diary, Unger, *Noah Webster*, p. 130, says delegates with whom Webster met during the Convention included Abraham Baldwin, James Duane, Oliver Ellsworth, Thomas Fitzsimmons, Benjamin Franklin, William Samuel Johnson, Rufus King, William Livingston, James Madison, Roger Sherman, Edmund Randolph, and other "Convention Gentlemen." According to Unger, p. 131, in June an antifederalist editor of *Freeman's Journal* published an open letter to the convention, accusing Webster of creating "disorder, confusion and error."

frequent visits and dinners with convention delegates,[19] and the Convention adopted some of the proposals that Webster advanced there. Webster's *Sketches* are, however, arguably more important as a contemporary expression of political theory and of frustrations over the Articles of Confederation than as a constitutional blueprint.

The first essay focused on the "Theory of Government." Webster followed social contract theorists, especially France's Jean Jacques Rousseau, in this essay in which he traced the origins of government to the desire to protect life and property and in which he portrayed the people as sovereign and the executive branch as their servant. Although he clearly favored a strong unitary executive, he opposed an absolute executive veto and hereditary aristocracy – "a form of government of all others the most to be dreaded" (p. 16)[20] — in favor of representative democracy, which he suitably described not as a perfect system, but as "the most perfect system of government that is practicable on earth." (p. 11)

The second essay, which focused on "Governments on the Eastern Continent," like future discussions at the Constitutional Convention, canvassed a wide number of regimes from ancient Greece and Rome to Great Britain, Poland, Italy, Germany, the Swiss Cantons, Spain, and elsewhere. Webster was at once realistic about the flaws of human nature and human institutions – "All human institutions must be imperfect" (p. 11) – yet hopeful that the New World might escape the major flaws of the Old. Webster associated despotic governments with standing armies, the fear of external forces, and the use of superstitious religion as a prop. He also thought that "free government" required "*an*

20. For readers' convenience, the author has used internal page numbers to all references in the *Sketches*, rather than footnotes, and has modernized spellings, since readers can easily compare them to original spellings in the document that follows.

equal distribution of property" (p. 18), which he defined as inequality unrelated to "hereditary offices and dignities" (p. 18) Webster advocated fairer systems of popular representation in Great Britain, but he doubted that there was much that could be done in the short time to counter the long-standing inertia there and in the rest of Europe.[21]

In his third essay, Webster examined the constitutions of "American States." He observed that American constitutions had been "framed in the most enlightened period of the world." (p. 23) He was especially complimentary of the constitutions of the New England states in general and his home state of Connecticut in particular. He regretted the slave trade and thought it could be abolished. He praised the elimination of hereditary distinctions and titles of nobility, and urged states to proceed on the road to disestablishment of religion, by, among other measures, eliminating requirements to profess Christianity to run for office and by eliminating limitations on public offices that clergymen could hold. He further argued that in societies, like those in America, which were thinly populated and where agriculture dominated, minds and other human faculties were expanded.

These reflections led to Webster's most important observations in his "Plan of Policy for improving the Advantages and perpetuating the Union of the American States." Like many other contemporary observers, Webster recognized that the primary weakness in the Articles of Confederation was the

21. By 1804, then a confirmed member of the Federalist Party, Webster had come to question some of the liberal optimism he had expressed in his first two essays. Writing to James Kent on October 20, he observed that "I find in the first parts many chimerical notions respecting a popular government which I had imbibed from the writings of Dr. Price and Rousseau." Quoted in V. P. Bynack, "Noah Webster's Linguistic Thought and the Idea of an American National Culture," *Journal of the History of Ideas* 45 (January-March, 1984), p. 101.

weakness of Congress vis-à-vis the states. The existing confederation was but "a cob-web." (p. 32) The idea, embodied in Article II of the Articles, that each state would preserve its sovereignty and independence, was "a solecism in politics that will sooner or later dissolve the pretended union, or work other mischiefs." (p. 33) Webster believed that one could fashion the relation between Congress and the states after that of a state, like Connecticut, to its municipalities, where the state would take care of common concerns and the subdivisions would deal with police matters.[22] Webster observed: "As towns and cities are, as to their small matters, sovereign and independent, and as to their general concerns, mere subjects of the state; so let the several states, as to their own police, be sovereign and independent, but as to the common concerns of all, let them be mere subjects of the federal head." (p. 35)[23]

This is certainly an intimation of the federal system that the Convention adopted but hardly a blueprint. Significantly, in this pamphlet Webster had not advocated, although he later supported, a bicameral Congress; he described judges as part of the executive branch; he appears to have anticipated continuing equal state representation in Congress; and, in the *Sketches*, Webster supported annual elections.

---

22. Walter H. Bennett, "Early Theories of Federalism," *The Journal of Politics* 4 (August, 1942), p. 391, cites Pelatiah Webster, Noah Webster, and the pseudonymous "Tullius" as individuals prior to the Convention who "supported the theory that sovereignty was divided when federal unions were created out of previously independent states."

23. In a footnote, p. 35, Webster added an analogy based on the relation between the moon and the earth and the planets and the moon. Perhaps not coincidentally, Madison reports that, in arguments on June 7 at the Constitutional Convention, John Dickinson "compared the proposed National System to the Solar System, in which the States were the planets, and ought to be left to move freely in their proper orbits." See Farrand, *The Records of the Federal Convention of 1787*, I, 153. Pennsylvania's James Wilson was impressed enough with the analogy that he responded, I, 153, that "He was not however

Webster was especially interested in vesting Congress with adequate power over taxation and commerce. He thought it essential to grant Congress the power to compel compliance with its laws, presumably by acting directly (as in the Constitution that the Convention adopted) on individual citizens. He referred to the idea of governing by "*resolves* and *recommendations*" as "a ridiculous farce, a burlesque on government, and a reproach to America." (p. 44)

Tackling an issue that the Convention would leave to the states but that Webster would champion throughout his own long life, Webster advocated education as a way of diffusing knowledge throughout the United States and of reducing local prejudices. Further addressing another issue that the Convention addressed only around the edges,[24] Webster favored the abolition of slavery.

Ultimately, Webster wanted citizens of the thirteen states to act as citizens of a single nation. He observed that "We ought not to consider ourselves as inhabitants of a particular state only; but as Americans; as the common subjects of a great empire." (p. 43)

IV.

Webster reiterated his support for the Constitution after the Convention when on October 17, 1787, he published "An Examination into the Leading Principles of the Federal Constitution," under the pseudonym "A Citizen of America."[25]

---

for extinguishing these planets . . . neither did he on the other hand, believe that they would warm or enlighten the Sun."

24. Paul Finkelman, *Slavery and the Founders: Race and Liberty in the Age of Jefferson* (Armonk, NY: M.E. Sharpe, 1996).

25. This work is found in *The Debate on the Constitution: Federalist and Antifederalist Speeches, Articles, and Letters During the Struggle Over Ratification,*

at Mount Sinai," he portrayed the document as the creation of "an *empire of reason*."[26] He defended dividing Congress into two houses, denied that the institution of the new government would eliminate the state legislatures, rejected the need for a bill of rights or a prohibition of standing armies, supported congressional taxing powers, supported the new judicial system, and, despite his own anti-slavery sentiments, even accepted the convention's decision not to put an immediate end to the slave trade.

Consistent with his *Sketches*, Webster argued that "The present situation of our American states is very little better than a state of nature."[27] Also reflecting earlier themes, Webster praised the widespread distribution of property in America, favored widespread education, and praised popular elections. Encouraging readers to focus on the "many sacrifices made to the general interest," he encouraged them not to censure "the small faults" that they might perceive in the new document.[28]

Writing as "Giles Hickory" in the *American Magazine* (which he edited and published in New York) in December, 1787, Webster further expanded on his opposition to a Bill of Rights. Clearly not opposed to the fundamental rights at issue, Webster thought both that such bills were unnecessary where the legislature represented the people and that there was impropriety in attempting to design

---

2 Parts (New York: The Library of America, 1993), Part I, pp. 129-63. Although the practice of using a pen name was not unusual, he apparently did so in this case because he had alienated numerous readers by his earlier attack on Shay's Rebellion.

26. *Ibid.*, I, 129. In *Federalist* No. 1, Alexander Hamilton observed that "It has been frequently remarked that it seems to have been reserved to the people of this country, by their conduct and example, to decide the important question, whether societies of men are really capable or not of establishing good government from reflection and choice, or whether they are forever destined to depend for their political constitutions on accident and force. See Alexander Hamilton, James Madison, and John Jay, *The Federalist Papers*, ed. Clinton Rossiter (New York: New American Library, 1961), p. 33.

27. *Ibid.*, I, 154.

28. *Ibid.*, I, 162.

"unalterable" constitutions.[29] Somewhat surprisingly for a journalist, Webster was even wary of embodying protection for "*liberty of the Press*" within the new document.[30]

Even before the Constitution had been proposed, Webster had been using his school texts and his dictionaries to provide the cultural unity that the Constitution tried to secure through political means. In this respect, he played a role equivalent to that of many of the Founding Fathers who actually attended the Constitutional Convention of 1787 and contributed to the writing of the Constitution. Before these delegates arrived in Philadelphia as representatives of individual states, Webster reminded them that they represented a larger whole. As voters considered the constitution the Constitutional Convention had produced, he urged them to focus not on their individual objections but on the general good it could achieve.

V.

Webster's life was a life of continuing publication and public service. He edited a daily newspaper in New York entitled *American Minerva*, along with a semiweekly *Herald*. He subsequently resumed the practice of law for a time in New Haven but again became engrossed in his writings. Moving to Amherst in 1812, he helped found Amherst College and was an advocate of numerous reforms.

Frustrated by the continuing advantages that slaves – who were counted as three-fifths of a person for purposes of representation in the U.S. House of Representatives and thus indirectly in calculating representation in the electoral college – gave to the

29. This essay may be found in *Ibid.*, at I, 669-72. The specific quotation is from p. 670.
30. See his "Reply to the Pennsylvania Minority: 'America,'" which he published in the New York *Daily Advertiser* on December 31, 1787. This is found at *Ibid.*, I, 553-62. The specific quotation is from I, 556. As an ardent Federalist, Webster later supported the Sedition Act of 1798, adopted during the Administration of John Adams, which made it a crime to criticize the government or the president. See Unger, *Noah Webster*, pp. 232-33.

southern states and cognizant of the throes of economic dislocation in New England brought about by embargoes and the War of 1812, Webster was among those who led the call in 1814 for the Hartford Convention. Although he was not selected to attend, he submitted a series of eleven proposals for constitutional change, which included apportioning taxes according to free population, limiting embargoes to sixty days, restricting the admission of new states into the Union (which, he thought, was increasing southern strength), and limiting presidents to a single term.[31] Had more radical voices prevailed, this Convention could have dissolved the union that Webster had helped forge. Fortunately, it did not succeed, and Andrew Jackson's victory in New Orleans resulted in a resurgent nationalism that enabled the nation to remain together until it was torn by the outbreak of the Civil War (and the slave interests against which Webster had warned through much of his life) in 1861.

In the interim, Webster pressed toward his earlier vision. Although he had previously published shorter dictionaries, in 1828 he finally published the 70,000 word *American Dictionary of the English Language*, on which he had begun work in 1812. In preparing this work, Webster had learned the rudiments of at least twenty languages and traveled to England and France to do library research. Although the work did not prove to be a financial success in Webster's own life-time (the Merriam brothers would later pay the family $250,000 when they renewed the copyright of a revised edition),[32] critics recognized that it was superior to any such previous work, and its publication did much to establish America as a distinct English-speaking entity.

---

31. Unger, *Noah Webster*, p. 280. Webster explained his own role in this event in his "Origin of the Hartford Convention in 1814," in Webster, *Collection of Papers*, 1968 reprint, pp. 311-15.

Webster was not the only former supporter of the Constitution who advocated this Convention. Gouverneur Morris, a New Yorker who had represented Pennsylvania at the Convention and who had given the final polish to the Constitution, also did so. See Richard Brookhiser, *Gentleman Revolutionary, Gouverneur Morris: The Rake Who Wrote the Constitution* (New York: Free Press, 2003), p. 202.

Webster had been a consistently religious man even before he had undergone a conversion experience in 1808, but he had removed Bible readings from his school books for fear that children would become too cavalier toward them. He published a revised edition of the Bible in 1833 (one of his innovations was to decrease the direct mentions of God). Despite his efforts on this project, it too had little commercial success.

Noah Webster died in 1843 at New Haven, where he had returned to live about 20 years before. He is buried in the New Haven Grove Street Cemetery next to Yale University, where his wife Rebecca Greenleaf, mother of their eight children, joined him in 1847. In 1936, his New Haven house was moved to the Greenfield Village in Dearborn, Michigan, where it remains a tourist site.

Unlike *The Federalist* and other contemporary works that have been continually reprinted throughout American history, Webster's *Sketches* have not. This facsimile edition, which thus reproduces the original shift in type in the last six pages, is only the second to have been printed in book form.[33] The first was appropriately published at the time of the sesquicentennial of the writing of the U.S. Constitution in 1937.[34] In similarly appropriate fashion, this edition will be published on the eve of the 250th anniversary of Webster's birth.

John R. Vile
March 2007

---

32. Unger, *Noah Webster*, p. 341.

33. Warfel, 1937, p. iii, records that the *Sketches* had been printed "in whole or in part," in *The State Gazette* of South Carolina in 1786, in *The Maryland Gazette* or *Baltimore Advertiser* in 1785 and 1786, and in the *Daily Advertiser: Political Historical, and Commercial*, of New York in 1786. He also reports that the last sketch was published in Volume VIII, No. 197 of *Old South Leaflets* [1908?].

34. The mistake is relatively inconsequential, but Warfel, 1937, p. i, incorrectly tied it to the sesquicentennial of the "adoption of the Constitution," which occurred, among agreeing states, not in 1787, when the Convention drafted it and 39 of 42 delegates present (one *in absentia*) signed it, but in 1788, when the ninth state —the majority specified as required in Article VII of the new Constitution — ratified.

SKETCHES

OF

American Policy.

Under the following Heads:

I. Theory of Government.

II. Governments on the Eastern Continent.

III. American States; or the principles of the American Constitutions contrasted with those of European States.

IV. Plan of Policy for improving the Advantages and perpetuating the Union of the American States.

By NOAH WEBSTER, Jun'r. Esq.

HARTFORD:
PRINTED BY HUDSON AND GOODWIN
M.DCC.LXXXV.

ADVERTISEMENT.

BEFORE the appearance of Dr. Price's Pamphlet, I had formed a design of publishing some Remarks on the American Constitutions and on the Federal Government. Many of my observations, particularly on religious tests and establishments, and on liberty of discussion, have been anticipated by that respectable writer, so distinguished by the justness and liberality of his sentiments and by his attachment to America. If the following observations, thrown together in haste and without much regard to method, can have any merit, it is this, that they are dictated by an honest intention and full conviction of their truth.

Sketches of American Policy.

Theory of Government.

MEN, in every ſtage of ſociety, have found it neceſſary to eſtabliſh ſome form of government to protect their perſons and property from invaſion.

Mankind may be conſidered in a threefold view—with reſpect to themſelves as individuals—with reſpect to the whole community or ſupreme power—and with reſpect to the magiſtrate or executive authority.

Every individual in ſociety has certain powers, rights and privileges, which no other individual can juſtly abridge or deſtroy; and of which conſequently the whole body of individuals has no right to deprive him without his conſent. But in a ſtate of nature, where every individual has rights, and has no power but his own ſtrength to defend them, his perſon is conſtantly expoſed to the abuſes, and his property, to the encroachments of his more powerful neighbour. Hence the origin of a ſocial compact which either expreſſed or implied, is the baſis of all civil government. This compact is nothing more than an aſſociation of all the members of a community, by which each individual, for his own ſecurity, conſents to obey the general voice. This aſſociation of all the individuals of a community is called the *body politic* or *ſtate*. This body, when active, is called a *ſovereignty*; when compared with other ſtates, it is called ſimply a *power*. The members, ſpoken of collectively, are called *people*; ſpoken of ſeverally, they may be called *citizens*; and each member, being under the controul of the whole body, is, in this reſpect, a *ſubject*.

In this act of aſſociation, there is a reciprocal engagement between the public body and its particular members. The public body engages to protect the perſon and property of each member, and each member engages to be obedient to the public body. In other words, each individual engages to aſſiſt his fellow citizens in protecting the rights of the whole, merely from a regard to his own ſafety; and each engages to yield obedience to the public voice from the ſame motive. Hence we may obſerve that what is called *patrictiſm* or *public ſpirit* is nothing but ſelf-intereſt, acting in conjunction with other intereſts for its *own ſake*; and that *public good* is but the aggregate ſum of the individual intereſts, in a ſtate. Thus a ſtate, compoſed of ten thouſand individual intereſts, becomes, with reſpect to other ſtates, one ſingle intereſt and is conſidered as an individual.

A ſtate thus formed by compact is a ſovereign power and has a right to command the ſervices and obedience of each member. Should a queſtion ariſe, Whether ſuch a ſtate can exerciſe acts of tyranny? I anſwer, that it is impoſſible. The ſovereign power is the whole body of the people collectively, and the people will never make laws oppreſſive to themſelves. The whole body may be wrong in a political meaſure; but whenever this happens, it is always through miſtake and never through deſign. Inſtances of error in a ſtate are very rare and wrong meaſures always produce inconveniences which, if very obvious, ſoon find a remedy. When therefore the ſovereign power reſides in the whole body of the people, it cannot be tyrannical, not becauſe it is barred by a phyſical neceſſity, but becauſe the ſame power which frames a law, ſuffers all its conſequences, and no individual or collection of individuals will knowingly frame a law

law injurious to itself. In the social compact, every individual enters into an engagement with himself—in the laws of the public body, each member lays an obligation upon himself—and in obeying those laws, each yields obedience to himself. In such a state, every member is as much bound by the laws, as he is by a bond subscribed by his own hand, These principles apply, with equal force, to representative governments. When, agreeably to the constitution, a hundred men choose one person to represent them in enacting laws, they give him all their own power; he is their agent and substitute; his voice is the voice of his constituents; his consent to a measure is as binding upon the hundred as their own.

Let us see how these principles affect the rights of property. Every individual has some property, which, while it remains in him, is sacred and cannot be touched by the public. But every individual, when he becomes a part of the *body politic*, voluntarily relinquishes so much of his property as is necessary to defray the expence of securing the remainder. The public therefore has a right to call upon every individual for this proportion. But the public has no right to the property of a partial number of individuals, any more than a robber has a right to my purse because he has most strength; yet the public has a right to the property of the whole, whenever the general safety demands it.

In order to understand this clearly, it is necessary to define the term, *law*. *Law* is a rule or decree of the supreme power of a state, which respects all its members. Its object must be general, or it cannot be termed, *law*. The decrees of a supreme power must be general, and are therefore *laws*; for which reason, any acts which regard a part of the community, are unjust, unless where such power acts as a magistrate in subordination to law. Thus the supreme power cannot order a single person to do a tower of militia duty; yet it can call forth every effective man in the state. The supreme power cannot oblige an individual to fill a certain office; yet it can pass a law, creating such an office, and exacting a penalty ty of hundreds that refuse to accept it, when legally chosen. And when the supreme power chooses a person for any office, it acts wholly in subordination to law. The sovereign power has no right to tax an individual; but it has a right to tax all the individuals of the state, with any sums that the public safety requires.

The essence of sovereignty consists in the general voice of the people. But each individual pursues his own interest; and consults the good of others no farther than his own interest requires. Hence the necessity of *laws* which respect the whole body collectively, and restrain the pursuits of individuals when they infringe the public rights. But laws in the hands of people at large can have no energy. A law in the hands of a whole people, would have no more effect, than the principles of natural justice have among wild savages. Every individual would still be at liberty to obey or disobey that law at pleasure. Hence arises a third relation among a people, viz. that of the magistracy, the business of which is to execute those laws which the people enact in capacity of sovereign.

A people cannot divest themselves of the sovereignty, and when they choose a magistrate or governor, they appoint only a *servant* to execute their orders. Whenever an executive officer exceeds the limits of his duty or ventures to administer justice upon any rules or principles of his own, he encroaches on the sovereign power—he becomes a tyrant—and forfeits his life. But while he is invested with the power of executing the laws, he is a *public* servant; not, as some people foolishly imagine, a servant of any individual, but a servant of the state and responsible for his conduct to the sovereign power.

From the preceding considerations, it follows, that there are three distinct relations subsisting in a well organized society; the relation of citizens to each other as individuals; the relation of each citizen to the whole collectively or sovereign power; and the relation of each to the magistracy or executive authority. Every individual has a share of the sovereign power—every individual

dual

dual is a ſubject of that power—and a few only, who are public ſervants, are veſted with the right of adminiſtring the laws.

The people in their collective capacity, enact laws; the magiſtrates receive the laws from them with the power of the whole body to enforce them; and the people, in their individual capacities, yield obedience to the laws. On a due obſervance of theſe reſpective rights and duties depend the peace and happineſs of government: If the ſupreme power would *execute* laws; if the magiſtrates would *enact* them and the ſubjects refuſe to *obey* them, diſorder would ſucceed and deſpotiſm or anarchy be the fatal conſequence. The only inſtance in which the ſupreme power ought to interpoſe in enforcing its own decrees, is when the magiſtracy is inſufficient for the purpoſe; and ſuch want of power in the magiſtracy may ever be conſidered as a defect in the conſtitution.

In order to determine whether it is beſt to veſt the adminiſtration of the laws in one man or more, it is neceſſary to examine the ſubject with more attention.

Let us ſuppoſe we live in a ſociety conſiſting of a thouſand members. Theſe, in their collective capacity, form the ſupreme power, of which each member poſſeſſes a thouſandth part. If the executive power is veſted in all the members equally, each poſſeſſes a thouſandth part; which is ſo ſmall a proportion, that no individual can execute a law, and the probability is that the whole will never unite. Such a diviſion of power would deſtroy its effect. Suppoſing ten men of the thouſand are choſen as magiſtrates to execute the laws of the ſtate, in this caſe the power of the whole thouſand is veſted in ten men and the laws may be executed; but as there is ſtill a diviſion of power, the adminiſtration will be ſlow and feeble. Let the power of the whole be brought to a point and veſted in a ſingle perſon, and the execution of laws will be vigorous and deciſive.

If the ſociety is encreaſed to the number of ten thouſand ſubjects; each member then poſſeſſes but a ten thouſandth part of the ſovereignty, to which he is as much

ſubject

subject as an individual in the society of a thousand members. Hence it follows that in proportion as the number of citizens is encreased, the liberty of each is diminished. In a small parish an individual has a great proportion of influence; but in a large state, a single voice is almost lost among the multitude. If these propositions are true, it follows that the less proportion each will bears to the will of the whole, the less influence will manners have in preserving the peace of society; and of course the force of laws must be augmented in proportion. But as the opportunities for magistrates to abuse their power are multiplied in proportion to the magnitude of the state, the power of the legislature to restrain and punish the magistrates ought to be encreased in the same proportion.

If the influence of manners in regulating society, is diminished in proportion to the magnitude of a state, and the force of laws ought to be increased in the same ratio, it follows that the larger a state is, the less ought to be the number of magistrates.

To understand this maxim, we must consider that three different interests center in the person of the magistrate; his own private interest, tending solely to his own advantage; the interest of the magistracy, tending to the advantage of that body; and the interest of the whol e people collectively or the supreme power. In a perfect system of government, the interest of the individual should have *no* influence in administration; that of the magistracy should be *very inconsiderable*, and that of the people should govern all others. But such is the nature of man, that the public interest has the least influence; the interestof the magistracy is more powerful; and the interest of the individual bears the principal sway. This order is totally repugnant to the happiness of civil government. If a society is composed of a thousand individuals and the magistrates are ten, the interest of the individual in any one magistrate, is in fact but a thousandth part of the whole and that of the magistacy but a tenth, and yet his own interest will have the principal sway.

While

While theſe intereſts are divided, government muſt of courſe be feeble. Unite them and government becomes active and energetic. Suppoſe the executive power all veſted in an individual; the whole intereſt of the magiſtracy is blended with that of the individual; and this union of the two moſt active principles, renders government as energetic as poſſible. Hence we deduce the foregoing maxim that the number of magiſtrates ought to be in an inverſe proportion to the magnitude of the ſtate, the conſequence of which is that a monarchical form of government is beſt for large ſtates.

From the foregoing principles, we may learn what forms of government are moſt favourable for the liberty of the ſubject. No perſon can be ſaid to enjoy civil liberty, who has no ſhare in legiſlation, and no perſon is ſecure in ſociety, unleſs the laws are known and reſpected.

In deſpotic governments, where the ſceptre is ſwayed by an individual, the ruler, whether denominated an Emperor, a King or a Baſhaw, having the ſole right of making and executing laws, is the only perſon who enjoys any liberty. Every individual within his dominions is a ſlave. In this caſe, the intereſt of the individual, of the magiſtrate, and of the ſupreme power, are all united, and government is of courſe as active as poſſible. Hence the vigour and deciſion of military operations, when the power of the general is without limitation.

Deſpotic power is not always tyrannical; in the hands of a mild prince, it may be favourable to the rights of the ſubject. But ſuch is the depravity of human nature, that it is madneſs in a people to veſt ſuch power in an individual. Denmark furniſhes the only inſtance of abſolute power conferred on an individual by the ſolemn act of the people; and it furniſhes perhaps the only inſtance of abſolute power that has not been abuſed.

A limited monarchy, where the power of the ſovereign is reſtrained by certain laws, is far preferable to deſpotiſm. But monarch has the power of making *any* laws, the people are ſo far ſlaves. However ſuch power may be sanctified by time, custom or hereditary succession, the exercise of it, in a single instance, is an act of tyranny. The king of Great-Britain cannot make a single law binding upon his subjects, but he can defeat every bill that is proposed by parliament. Is such a nation free? The English boast of their privileges, and with some reason, when they draw a comparison between themselves and the vassals of a Polish nobleman. But when compared with the eternal immutable rights of man, their privileges shrink into insignificance. With what face can a nation boast of their liberties, when an individual of that nation can, with a single expression, *the king will consider of it*, defeat any measure that the parliament may adopt? Neither the title nor the dignities of royalty can make a king more honest or less fallible than another man; and upon the principles of natural right, any member of parliament might as well negative an act of that body, as the king. A nation which is subject to the will of an individual is a nation of slaves; whether that nation receives its laws from the arbitrary will of its sovereign, or whether the people reserve to themselves the right of making their own laws and give their sovereign full power to annihilate them at pleasure. In either case a nation is at the mercy of an individual*.

An aristocracy is a form of government of all others the most to be dreaded; I mean, where the right of legislation is vested in a hereditary nobility. The idea of being *born* a *legislator*, is shocking to common sense, and the fact is a reproach to human nature. In such a government, the interest of the people is out of question. The interest of the supreme power, of the magistracy, and of the individual are here blended, and they are distinct and independent of the interest of the people. The consequence is, that when these interests coincide in

* The sole exclusive right of levying taxes is vested in the house of commons; and is the only constitutional privilege of legislation in the English nation; unless we rank the right of dethroning and electing their king for male-administration, among their constitutional privileges.

in all the members of the legiflature, they are combined to oppreſs their ſubjects, and when they claſh, as often happens, the ſtate is torn with diſſenſions and civil war.

From the preceding conſideration, I deduce this definition of the moſt perfect practicable ſyſtem of government; "a government, where the right of *making* laws, is veſted in the greateſt number of individuals, and the power of *executing* them, in the ſmalleſt number." In large communities, the individuals are too numerous to aſſemble for the purpoſe of legiſlation; for which reaſon, the people appear by ſubſtitutes or agents; perſons of their own choice. A repreſentative democracy ſeems therefore to be the moſt perfect ſyſtem of government that is practicable on earth.

Governments on the Eaſtern Continent.

IT will be ſaid that I have deſcribed a ſyſtem of government, excellent in theory, but impracticable.

It will be alledged that all kinds of government have been attempted by mankind, and that all the efforts of knowledge and virtue have proved ineffectual to preſerve the rights of men from the graſp of ambition or from the gradual approaches of corruption.

I will not undertake to aſſert that a perfect ſyſtem of civil polity can be eſtabliſhed on earth. All human inſtitutions muſt be imperfect. Nor will I venture to predict, that a form of government, founded on the true principles of natural right; on the broad baſis of civil and religious liberty, can be permanent in the fluctuation of human events. But I dare aſſert that no nation, of which hiſtory gives us any account, was ever in a ſituation to make the experiment; and that there is nothing in the nature of things to render ſuch an event impoſſible.

To prove this it will be necessary to take a general view of the constitutions of government that have been most famous, either for their principles, their continuance, or their effects upon the happiness of society.

The three original principles which have operated generally to preserve union and subordination in society, are, the power of a standing army, the fear of an external force, and the influence of religion. In despotic governments, under which nine tenths of the human race are included, a standing army, at the command of the sovereign, has been generally established, for the purpose of enforcing obedience to his arbitrary edicts. It is extremely difficult, if not impossible, for a monarch to support his authority and maintain tranquility in his dominions, for any long period, without a military force. There is something in the idea of such a government repugnant to the feelings of mankind; and a people must be totally depressed by servitude and stupified by ignorance, not to feel a perpetual disposition to rebel. Besides, there is such an unconquerable inclination in human nature, unchecked by fear, to be supercilious and tyrannical, that few monarchs have swayed the sceptre for a long time, without giving their subjects the most justifiable grounds for insurrection.

In order therefore to secure the obedience of subjects, the terrors of religion have always been called in to aid the civil power, and in most countries, have been incorporated with the political institutions. It has been the policy of the sovereign to keep his subjects in ignorance, to teach them a blind obedience to the oracles of some deity, commonly fabricated or feigned by human contrivance, to impress their minds with the belief that their rulers and priests were beings of a superior order, who had some intercourse with their gods and had power to punish disobedience with the severest judgments. All the events of the natural world, earthquakes, thunder and lightning, eclipse, storms and famine, with the whole catalogue of imaginary prodigies, miracles, dreams, tricks of magic, and fabulous stories of demons, have been converted, by power and artifice, into instruments of tyranny. Thus mankind have been deluded from age to age and rendered subservient to the caprice, the pleasure and the ambition of their sovereigns.

These two instruments of despotism, superstition and a military force, command peace and subordination in all the kingdoms and empires on the eastern continent. Some states, both in antient and modern times, have been united by the fear of an external force. The states of Greece were obliged to combine for their mutual safety against the Persians; but when delivered from a foreign invasion, they were distracted with civil wars. Rome was never free from faction and tumult, for a long period, unless she was invaded or her armies were employed in foreign conquests. The Helvetic body was formed and is still preserved by the danger of conquest. Composed of several states, differing in religion and principles of government, and inhabited by a hardy race of men, there is no reason to suppose that their union could be of long duration, without a dread of falling victims to the house of Bourbon or Austria.

The same principle united the American States and answered, during the period of danger, all the purposes of a vigourous government.

It will be observed that I have not mentioned the influence of a wise system of laws and a regular administation, among the causes of peace and subordination. An established code of laws and tribunals of justice may prevent the crimes of individuals and small disturbances; but seldom or never prevent civil dissensions and we know of very few instances where the civil magistrate has been able, without the aid of a military force, to suppress a popular insurrection. On the contrary, history informs us, that those nations which have enacted the wisest systems of laws, and have been most distinguished for liberty and knowledge, have been the most frequenly involved in civil wars. This effect, however, is not the natural consequence of laws, science or freedom, but the inevitable consequence of defective constitutions. We ought always

always to keep in mind the material diſtinctions between the *conſtitution*, the *laws* and the *adminiſtration* of a government. Several nations, antient and modern, furniſh us with moſt excellent ſyſtems of law; all nations of any conſequence furniſh us with the moſt illuſtrious examples of upright, judicious magiſtrates; but hiſtory has not recorded a ſingle inſtance of a *wiſe conſtitution* of civil government. Singular as this aſſertion may appear, I believe it may be clearly demonſtrated.

To prove this fact, it is not neceſſary to mention deſpotic governments; theſe being ſo evidently an inverſion of the order of ſociety and an infraction of the ſacred rights of men, that they can have few advocates in America. I will make a few remarks on thoſe forms of government that have been moſt celebrated for freedom.

Much has been ſaid of the republics of Greece, Athens and Sparta. Their freedom, their valour, their diſintereſted patriotiſm, their literature, their arts, have been the ſubjects of endleſs panegyrick. But what were their governments? Before the days Solon and Lycurgus, their laws were extremely rude and barbarous. The ſupreme power was the people at large; who, being under no reſtraint, having no ſettled form of deliberation, and being at the ſame time illiterate and credulous, were generally at the command of ſome noiſy demagogue. In ſuch a popular aſſembly, it could not be expected that juſtice or policy would always direct the ſuffrages of the people. On the contrary, their public acts of legiſlation were capricious and irregular; guided by no rules and changed by every artful harangue. They would unanimouſly adopt a meaſure one day and as unanimouſly reſcind it the next, without any change of circumſtances. They would execrate and baniſh an illuſtrious perſonage, at the inſtigation of his artful enemy, and within a month, recal and receive him, with demonſtrations of joy, without any change in his character. In the early ages of Greece, her citizens were indeed free, but their freedom was licentiouſneſs. Solon and Lycurgus are celebrated as *lawgivers*; but they ought alſo to be condemned

demned as tyrants. They framed many wiſe regulations but they enacted cruel laws too, and impoſed them upon their countrymen with a rigour known only to arbitrary governments.

The ſame remarks will apply to the Roman ſtate. A banditti of robbers, who lived by plunder, founded the greateſt empire on earth. The firſt form of government which they eſtabliſhed, was the monarchical. On the abolition of monarchy, there aroſe a heterogeneous form of government, in which the interfering of oppoſite intereſts introduced every ſpecies of diſorder. The patricians or nobility, who were deſcendants of the antient ſenators, who formed a reſpectable council under the regal ſtate, claimed privileges diſtinct and ſuperior to the body of the people, who were denominated plebeians. Theſe two orders, conſtantly ſtruggling for prerogative and right, kept the Roman ſtate in a perpetual ferment. The plebeians were certainly right in maintaining their privileges; but as it ever happens in popular tranſactions, their phrenzy tranſported them at times beyond all bounds. The principles of the Gracchi were undoubtedly right, but they urged them too far and their noble attempts to ſave the rights of the people ended in bloodſhed. The *agrarian* law was founded on true principles of natural right; but it ſhould have been a part of the conſtitution; a different ſyſtem had prevailed and had become too firmly eſtabliſhed to be overthrown by any means but the ſword.

A ſtate where there are two diſtinct orders of men, one claiming hereditary honours and offices, can not with propriety be called a *republic*, or free government. Such a ſtate, when the rights of each order are preciſely defined and aſcertained in the conſtitution and when the privileges of a hereditary nobility, which are always encroachments on the natural rights of men, have been ſanctified by long poſſeſſion, may enjoy tolerable tranquility under a prudent adminiſtration. But it was the misfortune of the Romans to have no eſtabliſhed conſtitution. There was no fixed line of diſcrimination between the ancient

cient privileges of the Patricians and the rights of the Plebeians. Hence the insolence of the former and the jealousy of the latter incessantly embroiled the state. Treaties and temporary concessions, with some attempts to compromise differences by a code of laws and the establishment of new officers among the Plebeians, had some effect in suspending the dissensions which from time to time disturbed the peace of the state. But no application of partial remedies can effect a radical cure in a disordered constitution. Excellent laws and a wise magistracy may paliate, but can never remove the disorders that proceed from defects in the original frame of government. The discord which rent the Roman state, was the inevitable, the necessary consequence of a constitutional seperation of interests; and could not cease, till these interests were blended together, or the interest of one party was annihilated or silenced by superior force. This last event took place in Rome. An ambitious general, at the head of a veteran army, which had been accustomed to conquer, destroyed the liberties of the people, in a single day, on the plains of Pharsalia. The privileges of the senate were apparently respected for several hundred years; but a standing army at the command of the emperor, in effect annihilated their power, and they gradually lost both their name and existence.

A similar progress is observable in all those states which have been called *free*, and which have been composed of different orders of men. In Rome the contest was long and attended with alternate advantages. In Spain, the power and artifice of Cardinal Ximenes, prime minister to Charles V. put an end to to the, libeties of the people, in the short period of a single reign. In France absolute power made more gradual advances, but was effectually established. In Sweden there have been several revolutions, and the last, which happened but a few years past, was in favour of monarchy. Denmark has been mentioned as a singular instance of a despotic government established by the solemn resolution of the people. In England there have been the most vigorous

gorous exertions in opposition to the encroachments of tyranny, and those exertions have been attended with the best success. But in defiance of all the efforts of a brave and enlightened nation, the body of the people is reduced to a situation, little or nothing superior to the vassalage of the neighbouring nations. The United Provinces, taught by fatal experience, the evils of a despotic government, framed on their emancipation from Spain, a constitution, distinguished by the most extraordinary jealousy. The supreme power, not being brought to a point, but remaining in sevaral seperate assemblies, is destitute of all energy. Their measures are always slow and commonly ineffectual. In cases of extreme danger, the states general have been obliged to infringe the constitution to save the provinces from ruin. And after all their jealousy, they have lost the rights of a free people, by their own folly; and their present form of government is a kind of divided commercial aristocracy, without the benefits of a popular representation or the security of an energetic administration.

The republics of Italy, if they ever enjoyed freedom, are now aristocracies, of the worst kind. Several cities of Germany have obtained and still preserve very extensive civil privileges, but their religious establishments have depressed the human mind. The present emperor, the most amiable and illustrious prince in Europe, not even excepting the generous Louis XVIth, is unfettering his subjects, and many material changes are already introduced into his dominions. But the subjects of the princes of the empire are the most abject slaves.

The form of government in some of the Swiss Cantons is aristocratical; in others, it is said to be republican. I am not sufficiently informed to determine in my own mind, whether the constitutions of any of these small states or of their allies, are founded on principles of equal liberty. From the most accurate accounts we have of their internal police, I believe we may venture to say, that some of these cantons and the city of Geneva, enjoy a greater share of civil and religious liberty, than any other state or kingdom on the eastern continent.

If these remarks on the several constitutions of civil government, ancient and modern, are allowed to be just, we are prepared to enumerate their general defects and the causes that have contributed to change their form to the monarchical or aristocratical, or to a mixture of both.

The great fundamental principle on which alone a free government can be founded and by which alone the freedom of a nation can be rendered permanent, is an *equal distribution of property*. The reverse of this, an unequal distribution of lands, has been the cause of almost all the civil wars that have torn society in pieces, from the infancy of the Roman republic down to the revolution in England. I here speak of that unequal division of property which is perpetual and to which are annexed certain hereditary offices and dignities. Commerce creates very great inequality of property; but as this inequality is revolving from person to person and entitles the possessor to no pre-eminence in legislation, it is not dangerous to the liberties of the rest of the state.

The first remarkable instance of the evils which flow from hereditary distinctions, we have exhibited in the history of Rome. This state, had we no other instance, would be a sufficient proof, that no freedom can be of long duration, and that no society can enjoy long tranquility, where hereditary honours and superiority of birth are claimed by one part of the members to the exclusion of the rest. But the whole history of modern Europe is but a continued confirmation of this truth.

By the establishment of *feuds* in all the territories conquered by the warlike nations of the north; that curious military system, which discovers the spirit of those barbarous tribes, and was well calculated to preserve their conquests; by the establishment of this system throughout Europe, the wretched inhabitants were chained in perpetual vassalage, from which neither power nor policy has been able to deliver a single state. The governments that were erected upon this system, were of the mixed kind; the monarchical and the aristocratical. The Barons,

rons, who were lords of the foil, and could command the fervice of their tenants when they pleafed, were originally the poffeffors of all the civil power. But it was the policy and the ambition of their kings to abridge their power and humble their pride. This could not be effected but by enlarging the privileges of the people and thus attaching them to the crown. In this manner and by the edge of the fword, the enormous power of the nobility was much circumfcribed in every Europen kingdom, except Poland; and in moft of them the people obtained a fhare in legiflation. In England, the people, fword in hand, obtained from king Stephen and the Barons, magna charta the great bafis of all the freedom that was ever enjoyed in that kingdom. Their fubfequent ftruggles were attended with much violence, but generally terminated in the acquifition of new privileges.

We have feen in what manner the people in all the kingdoms of Europe, have been divefted of their legiflative privileges. In England alone the people ftill poffefs a fhadow of legiflative importance. But how is the nation reprefented in parliament? Englifhmen themfelves anfwer this queftion. A few thoufands of the dregs of the people, whofe votes are fold to the higheft bidder, elect the members of that fupreme council of the nation. In fome boroughs, feven or eight electors choofe two members, and in London feven thoufand electors choofe but four reprefentatives. With fuch unequal reprefentation, no nation can enjoy real liberty, whatever may be their pretentions. But this is not the greateft evil. One part of the legiflature confifts of lords fpiritual and temporal, who fit in the houfe of peers by birth, by title, or by office. This branch of the legiflature can negative any bill propofed by the commons. Where then is the fupreme power of the people? Not to mention the abfurdity of blending the civil and the ecclefiaftical powers; two diftinct orders that ought never to be combined.

To complete this *glorious free conftitution*, a fingle perfon, ſon, cloathed with royality indeed, but neither wiſer nor better for his dignity, has full power to negative every act of parliament and diſappoint all the meaſures of national wiſdom.

Whenever a man or body of men eſtabliſh to themſelves a ſhare in government, independent of the people, and when they are no longer reſponſible for their conduct, a ſtate may bid adieu to its freedom. This was the caſe with almoſt all the ſtates of Europe. The Cortes of Spain, the parliaments of England and France, the ſtates of Denmark and Sweden, were all compoſed of different orders of men who claimed diſtinct privileges. The king, the nobility, the clergy, the burghers and the peaſants formed a motley legiſlature. The principles, the manners, the intereſts and the feelings of theſe orders were ſo diſcordant, that it was utterly impoſſible for them to act in concert, without frequent conceſſions on one ſide and the other, which muſt injure their rights or wound their pride. The prerogatives of a king, the inſolence of a baron or the bigotry of an eccleſiaſtic, have ſet whole nations butchering each other. Let a man read the hiſtory of the civil wars in France, the conteſt between the houſes of York and Lancaſter, and the uſurpation of Cromwell in England, and theſe alone will make him execrate the people who ever created or tolerated any diſtinction but that of merit, or that which is created or annihilated by their own voluntary choice.

Another moſt capital defect in all the pretended free governments of Europe, is the eſtabliſhment or preference, given to ſome religious perſuaſion. Next to the feudal ſyſtem, the eſtabliſhment of religions has done the moſt miſchief of any event or inſtitution on earth. Both theſe ſyſtems were united in the dark ages of Europe, and the terrors of ſuperſtition were added to the ſword of the civil magiſtrate, to depreſs the mind and bind the human race in extreme ſervitude.

I ſhall not mention the particular defects that are to be found in various conſtitutions of civil government. An unequal diſtribution of property, the perpetuity of

eſtates

estates, hereditary distinctions and offices, with religious establishments, are alone sufficient to destroy the liberties of a state and support any system of domination however absurd or oppressive. One or all of these evils are interwoven into every government in Europe, unless some of the cantons of Switzerland, or some small cities should be exceptions.

The reason why such absurd systems should ever have prevailed is doubtless this: The basis of every constitution of civil government on the eastern continent, was prelaid by barbarians, in whom the military spirit was predominant. The feudal system, a most excellent institution among savages who have neither money nor standing forces, but subversive of all the rights of civil society, was introduced into the southern provinces of Europe, by those martial tribes who overwhelmed the Roman empire. This distribution of property and the papal system of ecclesiastical tyranny, held Europe for several centeries in slavery and barbarism. Upon the revival of literature and the arts, the most violent efforts were made in every part of Europe to shake off the yoke. These efforts were productive of every species of calamity to mankind—civil wars, treachery and assassination · but they generally terminated in some acquisitions favourable to civil and ecclesiastical liberty. The power of a haughty nobility was abridged; the prerogatives of kings were ascertained; oppressive military tenures were abolished, and in their place were substituted rents that were certain and fixed by contract; while in some kingdoms the peasants obtained a share in legislation.

But however the rigours of the military services have been mitigated and some valuable religious rights have been acquired; still the effects of the feudal and papal systems are visible in all the European countries. It was impossible that such absurd and abusive systems could remain unattacked in the ages of intellectual improvement; but it is extremely difficult, if not impossible, to overthrow constitutions, generally established and grown venerable by time. All that Europeans can do, is to introduce

introduce gradual alterations, and from time to time make ſuch amendments as circumſtances will permit, and the rights of mankind require. But the rights of primogeniture, hereditary rights of legiſlation, and ſyſtems of religion eſtabliſhed by law, thoſe inſtitutions and cuſtoms that infringe all the ſacred rights of mankind, and reproach human nature, are perhaps become too cloſely connected with the peace of ſociety, to be aboliſhed, either by a ſingle ſtroke of power, or the gradual improvements of policy.

From the foregoing conſiderations, we may deduce with certainty this concluſion, that no ſociety of men has ever been in a ſituation to form a perfect or even an excellent ſyſtem of civil polity. All the governments of Europe, Aſia and Africa have been planned by rude uncivilized nations. Edifices built by ſuch unſkilful hands muſt be imperfect and uncouth. Modern architects may ſupply a pillar, cover a defect or add ornaments to ſuch an edifice; but they can neither render it convenient nor elegant, without raſing the whole ſtructure to the foundation.

From the foregoing remarks, we may likewiſe learn the propriety of diſtinguiſhing between the *laws* and the *conſtitution* of a ſtate. Engliſhmen ſeem to overlook this diſtinction and laviſh thoſe praiſes on their *glorious free conſtitution*, which are due to an excellent code of *laws*. That the Engliſh conſtitution is preferrable to that of Poland or of Spain, will not be diſputed; but the ſubjects of ſeveral monarchies on the continent, are happier, under a wiſe prince, than Engliſhmen have generally been with all their freedom. But thoſe defects which I have repeatedly mentioned in the courſe of theſe obſervations, which were introduced into England by its conquerors, are ſo interwoven into government, that they are gradually undermining and will eventually deſtroy all the liberty that remains in that kingdom. Commerce, which is the ſupport of liberty, will protract the period of deſpotiſm; but corruption and the power of ſome ambitious prince will ſome time or other put an end even

to

to their pretended privileges. Wise laws and an upright administration may correct temporary and accidental evils; but can never reform a fundamental error, as an anodyne will alleviate the pains of a disease; but will not effect a radical cure.

Thus the inhabitants of the eastern continent are mostly chained in vassalage—without knowledge, without freedom and without hope of relief.

American States.

THE theory of civil government and the general description of the kingdoms and states in Europe and Asia, which have been exhibited in the preceding pages, are designed as introductory to some remarks on the American states.

A tolerable acquaintance with history and a small knowledge of the English settlements on this continent, teach us that the situation of these states, is, in every point of view, the reverse of what has been the infant situation of all other nations.

In the first place, our constitutions of civil government have been framed in the most enlightened period of the world. All other systems of civil polity have been begun in the rude times of ignorance and savage ferocity; fabricated at the voice of necessity, without science and without experience. America, just beginning to exist in an advanced period of human improvement, has the science and the experience of all nations to direct her in forming plans of government. By this advantage she is enabled to supply the defects and avoid the errors incident to the policy of uncivilized nations; and to lay a broad basis for the perfection of human society. The legislators of the American states are neither swayed by a blind veneration for an independent clergy, nor

nor awed by the frowns of a tyrant. Their civil policy is or ought to be the result of the collected wisdom of all nations, and their religion, that of the Saviour of mankind. If they do not establish and perpetuate the best systems of government on earth, it will be their own fault, for nature has given them every advantage they could desire.

In the next place, an equal distribution of landed property, is a singular advantage, as being the foundation of republican governments and the security of freedom*. The New-England states are peculiarly happy in this respect. Lands descend equally to all the heirs of the deceased possessor and perpetuities are entirely barred. In Connecticut the eldest male heir inherits two shares; this is a relique of ancient prejudices in favour of

* Several writers on government and particularly the great Montesquieu, maintain that *virtue* is the foundation of republics. If, by virtue, is meant *patriotism*, or disinterested public spirit, and love of one's country, as is probably the case; with the utmost respect for such authorities, I must deny that such a general principle ever did or ever can exist in human society. Local attachments exist under every species of government. They are as strong in monarchies as in republics. *Honour*, which is said to be the principle of monarchical governments, is often as powerful a motive in republics. The real principle that is predominat in every individual and directs all his actions, is self-interest. This operates differently and takes different names, under different forms of government. In a democracy, where offices and preferment are at the disposal of the people, an ambitious man must court the people, by his condescention, by public acts of beneficence, and by pretentions to public good. In order to retain any emoluments, which he holds by the choice of the people, his conduct must be agreeable to them, and apparently, if not really for their interests. This conduct springs from self-love, but takes the name of *virtue* or *public spirit*. In a monarchy, where the sovereign disposes of posts of honour and profit, and where distinction of rank takes place, a candidate takes a different method to procure favour. He professes the most unshaken loyalty, and a firm attachment to the person of his sovereign; he assumes an air of dignity and shapes his conduct to the humour of the court. This is the same selfish principle, aiming at the same object; but operating in a different manner, it is denominated *honour*. But the existence, of any form of government does not depend on any principle of action, however modified, or by whatever name distinguished.

of the rights of primogeniture, which the wisdom of succeeding legislatures will undoubtedly abolish. An act passed the legislature of New-York, a few years past, destroying and barring entailments and ordering that all intestate estates should descend to all the heirs in equal portions. No act was ever better timed or calculated to produce more salutary effects. The states of Pennsylvania and North-Carolina have made it an article in their Constitutions, that no estates shall be perpetual. I am not sufficiently acquainted with the constitutions of the other states, to inform whether perpetuities are barred or not; but they may be avoided by a *common recovery*, a fiction often practised in the English courts of law.

But although the southern states possess too much of the aristocratic genius of European governments, yet it is probable that their future tendency will be towards republicanism. For if the African slave-trade is prohibited, it must gradually diminish the large estates which are entirely cultivated by slaves; as these will probably decrease without recruits from Africa. And it is not probable that their place can be supplied by white people, so long as vast tracts of valuable land are uncultivated; and poor people can purchase the fee of the soil.

But should the present possessors of lands continue to hold and cultivate them, still their is a new sett of men springing up in the back parts of those states; more hardy and independent than the peasants of the low countries; and more averse to aristocracy. The unhealthiness of the climate in the flat lands, is a circumstance that will contribute to the rapid population of the mountains where the air is more salubrious.

The idea therefore that the genius of the southern states is verging towards republicanism, appears to the supported by substantial reasons. It is much to be wished that such an idea might be well grounded, for nature knows no distinctions, and government ought to know none, but such as are merited by personal vertues.

The confiscation of many large estates in every part of the union, is another circumstance favourable to an equal diſtribution of property. The local ſituation of all the ſtates and the genius of the inhabitants in moſt of them, tend to deſtroy all the ariſtocratic ideas which were introduced from our parent country.

Neceſſarily connected with an equal diſtribution of landed property, is the annihilation of all hereditary diſtinctions of rank. Such diſtinctions are inconſiſtent with the nature of popular governments. Whatever pretentions ſome ſtates have made to the name of *republics*; yet thoſe that have permitted perpetual diſtinctions of property, and hereditary titles of honour with a right of legiſlation annexed, certainly never deſerved the name of popular governments; and they have never been able to preſerve their freedom. Wherever two or more orders of men have been eſtabliſhed with hereditary privileges of rank, they have always quarrelled till the power or intrigues of the ſuperior orders, have diveſted the people of all their civil liberties. In ſome countries they retain a ſhow of freedom, ſufficient to amuſe them into obedience; but in moſt ſtates, they have loſt even the appearance of civil rights.

Congreſs, aware of the tendency of an unequal diviſion of property and the evils of an ariſtocracy or a mixed form of government, have inſerted a clauſe in the articles of confederation, forever barring all titles of nobility in the American ſtates; a precaution evincive equally of the foreſight, the integrity and the republican principles of that auguſt body*.

Another

* The jealouſy even of the ſouthern ſtates in regard to the eſtabliſhment of rank and hereditary titles, was remarkable in the oppoſition which appeared againſt the Cincinnati. The original deſign of that ſociety, was not only harmleſs, but extremely laudable. It was a monument raiſed to the memory of an army which defended the nobleſt cauſe ever undertaken by man. But perhaps the plan involved in it conſequences which were not apprehended by the gentlemen who formed it. There is however ſome difficulty in conceiving how a mere title, without property and legiſlative rights, could endanger our liberties. Evil conſequences might reſult from ſuch a ſociety; but they muſt be extremely remote. It muſt require the continued efforts of ſeveral generations to accumulate a dangerous degree of power in a ſociety, conſiſting of few members, who would be ſcattered throughout the continent.

Another circumſtance, favourable to liberty and peculiar to America, is a moſt liberal plan of eccleſiaſtical policy. Dr. Price has anticipated moſt of my obſervations on this head. If ſound ſenſe is to be found on earth, it is in his reaſoning on this ſubject. The American conſtitutions are the moſt liberal in this particular of any on earth; and yet ſome of them have retained ſome badges of bigotry. A profeſſion of the chriſtian religion is neceſſary in the ſtates, to entitle a man to office. In ſome ſtates, it is requiſite to ſubſcribe certain articles of faith. Theſe requiſitions are the effect of the ſame abominable prejudices, that have enſlaved the human mind in all countries; which alone have ſupported error and all abſurdities in religion. If there are any human means of promoting a millenial ſtate of ſociety, the only means are a general diffuſion of knowledge and a free unlimited indulgence given to religious perſuaſions, without diſtinction and without preference. When this event takes place, and I believe it certainly will, the *beſt* religion will have the moſt advocates. Nothing checks the progreſs of truth like human eſtabliſhments. Chriſtianity ſpread with rapidity, before the temporal powers interfered; but when the civil magiſtrate undertook to guard the truth from error, its progreſs was obſtructed, the ſimplicity of the goſpel was corrupted with human inventions, and the efforts of Chriſtendom have not yet been able to bring it back to its primitive purity.

The American ſtates have gone far in aſſiſting the progreſs of truth; but they have ſtopped ſhort of perfection. They ought to have given every honeſt citizen an equal right to enjoy his religion and an equal title to all civil emoluments, without obliging him to tell his religion. Every interference of the civil power in regulating opinion, is an impious attempt to take the buſineſs of the Deity out of his own hands; and every preference given to any religious denomination, is ſo far ſlavery and bigotry. This is a blemiſh in our conſtitutions, reproachful in proportion to the light and knowledge of our legiſlators.

The

The general education of youth is an article in which the American ſtàtes are ſuperior to all nations. In Great Britain the arts and ſciences are cultivated to perfection; but the inſtruction of the loweſt claſſes of people is by no means equal to the American yeomanry. The inſtitution of ſchools, particularly in the New-England ſtates, where the pooreſt children are inſtructed in reading, writing and arithmetic, at the public expence, is a noble regulation, calculated to dignify the human ſpecies.

This inſtitution is the neceſſary conſequence of the genius of our governments; at the ſame time, it forms the firmeſt ſecurity of our liberties. It is ſcarcely poſſible to reduce an enlightened people to civil or eccleſiaſtical tyranny. Deprive them of knowledge, and they ſink almoſt inſenſibly in vaſalage. Ignorance cramps the powers of the mind, at the ſame time that it blinds men to all their natural rights. Knowledge enlarges the underſtanding, and at the ſame time, it gives a ſpring to all the intellectual faculties, which direct the deliberations of the cabinet and the enterprizes of the field. A general diffuſion of ſcience is our beſt guard againſt the approaches of corruption, the prevalence of religious error, the intrigues of ambition and againſt the open aſſaults of external foes.

In the ſouthern ſtates education is not ſo general*. Gentlemen of fortune give their children a moſt liberal education; and no part of America produces greater lawyers, ſtateſmen and divines; but the body of the people are indifferently educated. In New-England, it is

rare

* An officer of the New-York line, in the late war, who had an opportinity to be particularly acquainted with the New-England troops, has told me repeatedly, that he found the non-commiſſioned officers in the Connecticut line, better educated than the commiſſioned officers of the New-York troops. An officer in a Pennſylvania regiment, informed me that he found many officers of the line on their eſtabliſhment, who could not make out the regimental returns. The flouriſhing ſtate of South-Coralina never had an academy till within a few months paſt. I cannot learn that North-Carolina has yet any kind of college or academy. A few gentlemen ſend their ſons to Europe for an education.

rare to find a person who can not read and write; but if I am rightly informed, the case is different in the southern states. The education, however, of the common people in every part of America, is equal to that of any nation; and the southern states, where schools have been much neglected, are giving more encouragement to literature.

It is not my design to enumerate all the political and commercial advantages of this country; but only to mention some of the characteristic circumstances which distinguish America from all the kingdoms and states of which we have any knowledge.

One further remark however, which I cannot omit, is that the people in America are necessitated, by their local situation, to be more sensible and discerning, than nations which are limited in territory and confined to the arts of manufacture. In a populous country, where arts are carried to great perfection, the mechanics are obliged to labour constantly upon a single article. Every art has its several branches, one of which employs a man all his life. A man who makes heads of pins or springs of watches, spends his days in that manufacture and never looks beyond it. This manner of fabricating things for the use and convenience of life is the means of perfecting the arts; but it cramps the human mind, by confining all its faculties to a point. In countries thinly inhabited, or where people live principally by agriculture, as in America, every man is in some measure an artist—he makes a variety of utensils, rough indeed, but such as will answer his purpose—he is a husbandman in summer and a mechanic in winter—he travels about the country—he converses with a variety of professions—he reads public papers—he has access to a parish library and thus becomes acquainted with history and politics, and every man in New-England is a theologian. This will always be the case in America, so long as their is a vast tract of fertile land to be cultivated, which will occasion emigrations from the states already settled. Knowledge is diffused and genius roused by the very situation of America.

Plan

Plan of Policy for improving the Advantages and perpetuating the Union of the American States.

I HAVE already mentioned three principles which have generally operated in combining the members of society under some supreme power; a standing army, religion and fear of an external force. A standing army is necessary in all despotic governments. Religion, by which I mean superstition, or human systems of absurdity, is an engine used in almost all governments, and has a powerful effect where people are kept in ignorance. The fear of conquest is an infallible bond of union where states are surrounded by martial enemies. After people have been long accustomed to obey, whatever be the first motive of their obedience, there is formed a habit of subordination, which has an almost irresistible influence, and which will preserve the tranquillity of government, even when coercion or the first principle of obedience has ceased to operate.

None of the foregoing principles can be the bond of union among the American states. A standing army will probably never exist in America. It is the instrument of tyranny and ought to be forever banished from free governments. Religion will have little or no influence in preserving the union of the states. The christian religion is calculated to cherish a spirit of peace and harmony in society; but will not balance the influence of jarring interests in different governments. As to neighbouring foes, we have none to fear; and European nations are too wise or have too much business at home, to think of conquering these states.

We must therefore search for new principles in modelling our political system. The American constitutions are founded on principles different from those of all nations, and we must find new bonds of union to perpetuate the confederation.

In the firſt place, there muſt be a ſupreme power at the head of the union, veſted with authority to make laws that reſpect the ſtates in general and to compel obedience to thoſe laws. Such a power muſt exiſt in every ſociety or no man is ſafe.

In order to underſtand the nature of ſuch a power, we muſt recur to the principles explained under the firſt head of theſe obſervations.

All power is veſted in the people. That this is their natural and unalienable right, is a poſition that will not be diſputed. The only queſtion is, how this power ſhall be exerted to effect the ends of government. If the people retain the power of executing laws, we have ſeen how this diviſion will deſtroy all its effect. Let us apply the definition of a perfect ſyſtem of government to the American ſtates. "The right of making laws for the United Sates, ſhould be veſted in all their inhabitants by legal and equal repreſentation, and the right of executing thoſe laws, committed to the ſmalleſt poſſible number of magiſtrates, choſen annually by Congreſs and reſponſible to them for their adminiſtration." Such a ſyſtem of continental government is perfect—it is practicable—and may be rendered permanent. I will even venture to aſſert that ſuch a ſyſtem may have, in legiſlation, all the ſecurity of republican circumſpection; and in adminiſtration, all the energy and deciſion of a monarchy.

But muſt the powers of Congreſs be increaſed? This queſtion implies groſs ignorance of the nature of government. The queſtion ought to be, muſt the American ſtates be united? And if this queſtion is decided in the affirmitive, the next queſtion is, whether the ſtates can be ſaid to be united, without a legiſlative head? or in other words, whether thirteen ſtates can be ſaid to be united in government, when each ſtate reſerves to itſelf the ſole powers of legiſlation? The anſwer to all ſuch queſtions is extremely eaſy. If the ſtates propoſe to form and preſerve a confederacy, there muſt be a ſupreme head, in which the power of all the ſtates is united.

There

There must be a supreme head, clothed with the same power to make and enforce laws, respecting the general policy of all the states, as the legislatures of the respective states have to make laws binding on those states, respecting their own internal police. The truth of this is taught by the principles of government, and confirmed by the experience of America. Without such a head, the states cannot be *united*; and all attempts to conduct the measures of the continent, will prove but governmental farces. So long as any individual state has power to defeat the measures of the other twelve, our pretended union is but a name, and our confederation, a cobweb.

What, it will be asked, must the states relinquish their sovereignty and independence, and give Congress their rights of legislation? I beg to know what we mean by *United States*? If after Congress have passed a resolution of a general tenor, the states are still at liberty to comply or refuse, I must insist that they are not *united*; they are as *seperate*, as they ever were; and Congress is merely an advisory body. If people imagine that Congress ought to be merely a council of advice, they will some time or other discover their most egregious mistake. If three millions of people, united under thirteen different heads, are to be governed or brought to act in concert by a *Resolve, That it be recommended*, I confess myself a stranger to history and to human nature*. The very idea of uniting discordant interests and restraining the selfish and the wicked principles of men, by advisory resolutions, is too absurd to have advocates even among illiterate peasants. The resolves of Congress are always treated with respect, and during the late war, they were efficacious. But their efficacy proceeded from a principle of common safety which united the interests of all the states; but peace has removed that principle, and the states comply with or refuse the requisitions of Congress, just as they please.

The

* If the states cannot be brought to act in concert now, how can it be done when the number of the states is augmented and the inhabitants multiplied to many millions?

The idea of each ſtate preſerving its ſoveteignty and independence in their full latitude, and yet holding up the appearance of a confederacy and a concert of meaſures, is a ſolecism in politics that will ſooner or later diſſolve the pretended union, or work other miſchiefs ſufficient to bear conviction to every mind.

But what ſhall be done? what ſyſtem of government ſhall be framed, to guard our rights, to cement our union, and give energy to public meaſures? The anſwers to theſe queſtions are obvious and a plan of confederacy, extremely eaſy. Let the government of the United States be formed upon the general plan of government in each of the ſeveral ſtates. Let us examine the conſtitution of Connecticut.

The inhabitants of Connecticut form one body politic, under the name of the *Governor and Company of the State of Connecticut.* The whole body of freemen, in their collective capacity, is the ſupreme power of the ſtate. By conſent and firm compact or conſtitution, this ſupreme power is delegated to repreſentatives, choſen in a legal manner and duly qualified. Theſe repreſentatives properly aſſembled, make laws, binding on the whole ſtate; that is, the ſupreme power or ſtate makes laws binding on itſelf. The ſupreme power and the ſubjects of that ſupreme power are the ſame body of men. As a collective body, the citizens are all an individual; as ſeperate individuals, they are ſubjects as numerous as the citizens.

When laws are enacted they are of a general tenor; they reſpect the whole ſtate and cannot be abrogated but by the whole ſtate. But the whole ſtate does not attempt to execute the laws. The ſtate elects a governor or ſupreme magiſtrate and cloaths him with the power of the whole ſtate to enforce the laws. Under him a number of ſubordinate magiſtrates, ſuch as judges of courts, juſtices of the peace, ſheriffs, &c. are appointed to adminiſter the laws in their reſpective departments. Theſe are commiſſioned by the governor or ſupreme magiſtrate. Thus the whole power of the ſtate is brought to a ſingle point—it is united in one perſon.

If the representation of the freemen is equal, and the elections frequent; if the magistrates are constitutionally chosen and responsible for their administration, such a government is of all others the most free and safe*. The form is the most perfect on earth. While bills are depending before the supreme power, every citizen has a right to oppose them. A perfect freedom of debate is essential to a free government. But when a bill has been formally debated and is enacted into a law, it is the act of the whole state, and no individual has a right to resist it†.

But, as it has been before observed, the acts of the supreme power must be general, it has therefore by a general law delegated full authority to certain inferior corporations to make by-laws for the convenience of small districts and not repugnant to the laws of the state. Thus every town in Connecticut is a supreme power for certain purposes and the cities are invested with extensive privileges. These corporations, for certain purposes, are independent of the legislature; they make laws, appoint officers and exercise jurisdiction within their own limits. As bodies politic, they are sovereign and independent—as members of a large community, they are mere subjects. In the same manner, the head of a family, is sovereign in his domestic œconomy, but as a part of the state, he is a subject.

Let

* People, in the choice of rulers, are too apt to be deceived by an insinuating address and a specious show of popular virtues. I pretend not to lay down rules for other people; but for my own part, I will never give my vote to a man who courts my favour. I always suspect that such a man will be the first to betray me. Nor will I give my vote to men, merely because they *have been* in office and it will hurt their feelings to be neglected. Such motives appear to me to discover weakness and a disregard to the true principles of government. I endeavour to give my votes to men, in whose integrity and abilities I can repose confidence—men, who will not dispense with law and regid justice, to favour a friend or secure their own popularity. When I hear people talk of elevating a man to an office, because he comes *next in course*, and *he will do well enough*, I suspect they have forgot that they are freemen, and have lost their oaths or their consciences.

† To be the act of the whole state, an act should, strictly speaking, be assented to by every member; but this is often impossible; the act of the majority is therefore the most perfect and only practicable method of legislation.

Let a similar system of government be extended to the United States. As towns and cities are, as to their small matters, sovereign and independent, and as to their general concerns, mere subjects of the state; so let the several states, as to their own police, be sovereign and independent, but as to the common concerns of all, let them be mere subjects of the federal head. If the necessity of a union is admitted, such a system is the only means of effecting it. However independent each state may be and ought to be in things that relate to itself merely, yet as a part of a greater body, it must be a subject of that body, in matters that relate to the whole.

A system of continental government, thus organized, may establish and perpetuate the confederation, without infringing the rights of any particular state*. But the power of all the states must be reduced to a narrow compass—it must center in a single body of men—and it must not be liable to be controled or defeated by an individual state. The states assembled in Congress, must have the same compulsory power in matters that concern the whole, as a man has in his own family, as a city has within the limits of the corporation, and as the legislature of a state has in the limits of that state, respecting matters that fall within their several jurisdictions.

I beg to know how otherwise the states will be governed as a collective body? Every man knows by his own experience that even families are not to be kept in subordination by recommendations and advice. How much less then will such flimsy things command the obedience of a whole continent? They will not—they do not. A single state, by non-compliance with resolves of Congress, has repeatedly defeated the most salutary

* Such a form of Government resembles the harmony of nature in the planetary system. The moon is an inferior planet subject to the earth. The earth and other planets govern their secondary planets and at the same time, are governed by the sun, the common center of our system: And it is highly probable that the sun may be a planet, governed by some other great central body or power. A gradation, similar to this, is obvious in the animal world.

falutary meafures of the ftates, propofed by Congrefs and and acceded to by twelve out of thirteen†.

I will fuppofe for the prefent that a meafure, recommended by Congrefs and adopted by a majority of the legiflatures, fhould be really repugnant to the intereft of a fingle ftate, confidered in its feperate capacity. Would it be right for that ftate to oppofe it? While the meafure is in agitation it is the undoubted privilege of every ftate to oppofe it by every argument. But when it is paffed by the concurrence of a legal majority, it is the duty of every ftate to acquiefce.—So far from refifting the meafure, thofe very individuals, who oppofed it in debate, ought to fupport it in execution‡. The reafon is very plain—fociety and government can be fupported on no other principles. The intereft of individuals muft always give place to the intereft of the whole community. This principle of government is not perfect, but it is as perfect as any principle that can be carried into effect on this fide heaven.

It is for the intereft of the American ftates, either to be united or not. If their union is unneceffary, let Congrefs be annihiliated, or let them be denominated *a council of advice* and confidered as fuch. They muft then be ftripped of their power of making peace and war, and of a variety

† The manner in which the impoft of five per cent. has been prevented by the ftate of Rhode-Ifland is well known. It is a difgrace to any government on earth. That ftate has a local intereft in not complying with the meafure. A ftate impoft brings money into their treafury, but as that ftate imports more than it confumes, the duty on goods not confumed there, is clear gain. Thus a ftate by its local fituation is enabled to pay its debts and fupport government with money collected in the neighbouring ftates. If fuch a felfifh fyftem is fuffered to prevail, let us defolve the confederation, and let every ftate make the moft of its ftrength and advantages by filching from it neighbours. In fuch a game Rhode-Ifland will lofe.

‡ A delegate from Connecticut, who was in Congrefs when the half-pay refolution was debated, refolutely oppofed the meafure. But when it had legally paffed by a majority of voices, he acquiefced, and has ever defended the meafure; even at the hazard of his reputation. If there is any characteriftic of an honeft man and a good fubject, it is fuch a line of conduct.

variety of prerogatives given them by the articles of confederation. In this caſe we ourſelves and the ſtates of Europe, ſhould know what kind of a being Congreſs is —what dependence can be placed on their reſolves— what is the nature of the treaties which they have made and the debts they have contracted.

But if the ſtates are all ſerious in a deſign to eſtabliſh a permanent *union*, let their ſincerity; be evinced by their public conduct.

Suppoſe the legiſlature of Rhode-Iſland had no power to compel obedience to its laws, but any town in that ſtate had power to defeat every public meaſure. Could any laws be rendered effectual? Could it with propriety be called a ſtate? Could it be ſaid that there was any ſupreme power, or any government? certainly not. Suppoſe the ſmalleſt town in Connecticut had power to defeat the moſt ſalutary meaſures of the ſtate; would not every other town riſe in arms againſt any attempt to exert ſuch a power? They certainly would. The truth of the caſe is, where the power of a people is not united in ſome individual, or ſmall body of individuals, but continues divided among the members of a ſociety, that power is nothing at all. This fact is clearly proved under the firſt head of theſe obſervations, and more clearly felt by our fatal experience.

The American ſtates, as to their general internal police, are *not united*; there is no ſupreme power at their head; they are in a perfect ſtate of nature and independence as to each other; each is at liberty to fight its neighbour, and there is no ſovereign to call forth the power of the continent to quell the diſpute or puniſh the agreſſor†. It is not in the power of the Congreſs—they have no command over the militia of the ſtates—each ſtate commands its own, and ſhould any one be diſpoſed for

† Congreſs ordered a number of troops to be raiſed for taking poſſeſſion of the frontier poſts and defending them from the ſavages. A year has elapſed ſince this order and the troops are now moſtly at home. The enemy ſtill hold our forts, poſſeſs the furr trade and ravage our new ſettlements. Such weakneſs in government is infamy.

for civil war, the ſword muſt ſettle the conteſt and the weakeſt be ſacrificed to the ſtrongeſt.

It is now in the power of the ſtates to form a continental government, as efficacious as the interior government of any particular ſtate.

The general concerns of the continent may be reduced to a few heads; but in all the affairs that reſpect the whole, Congreſs muſt have the ſame power to enact laws and compel obedience throughout the continent, as the legiſlatures of the ſeveral ſtates have in their reſpective juriſdictions. If Congreſs have any power, they muſt have the whole power of the continent. Such a power would not abridge the ſovereignty of each ſtate in any article relating to its own government. The internal police of each ſtate would be ſtill under the ſole ſuperintendance of its legiſlature. But in a matter that equally reſpects all the ſtates, no individual ſtate has more than a thirteenth part of the legiſlative authority, and conſequently has no right to decide what meaſure ſhall or ſhall not take place on the continent. A majority of the ſtates *muſt* decide†; our confederation cannot be permanent, unleſs founded on that principle; nay more, the ſtates cannot be ſaid to be *united*, till ſuch a principle is adopted in its utmoſt latitude. If a ſingle town or precinct could counteract the will of a whole ſtate, would there be any government in that ſtate? It is an eſtabliſhed principle in government, that the will of the minority muſt ſubmit to that of the majority; and a ſingle ſtate or a minority of ſtates, ought to be diſabled to reſiſt the will of the majority, as much as a town or county in any ſtate is diſabled to prevent the execution of a ſtatute law of the legiſlature.

It is on this principle and *this alone*, that a free ſtate can be governed; it is on this principle alone that the American ſtates can exiſt as a confederacy of republics. Either the ſeveral ſtates muſt continue ſeperate, totally independent

† Congreſs have been more careful of our liberties; for the articles of confederation ordain, that, in matters of great national concern, the concurrence, not of *ſeven* ſtates, a mere majority, but of *nine* ſhould be requiſite to paſs a reſolution.

indedendent of each other, and liable to all the evils of jealouſy, diſpute and civil diſſention—nay, liable to a civil war upon any claſhing of intereſts; or they muſt conſtitute a general head, compoſed of repreſentatives from all the ſtates, and veſted with the power of the whole continent to enforce their deciſions. There is no other alternative. One of theſe events muſt inevitably take place, and the revolution of a few years will verify the prediction.

I know the objections that have been urged by the ſupporters of faction and perhaps by ſome honeſt men, againſt ſuch a power at the head of the ſtates. But the objections all ariſe from falſe notions of government or from a wilful deſign to embroil the ſtates. Many people, I doubt not, really ſuppoſe that ſuch power in Congreſs, would be dangerous to the liberties of the ſtates, Such ought to be enlightened.

There are two fundamental errors, very common in the reaſonings which I have heard on the powers of Congreſs. The firſt ariſes from the idea that our American conſtitutions are founded on principles ſimilar to thoſe of the European governments which have been called *free*. Hence people are led into a ſecond error; which is, that Congreſs are a body independent of their conſtituents and under the influence of a diſtinct intereſt.

But we have ſeen before that our ſyſtems of civil government are different from all others; founded on different principles, more favourable to freedom and more ſecure againſt corruption.

We have no perpetual diſtinctions of property, which might raiſe one claſs of men above another, and create powerful family connections and combinations againſt our liberties. We ſuffer no hereditary offices or titles, which might breed inſolence and pride, and give their poſſeſſors an opportunity to oppreſs their fellow men. We are not under the direction of a bigoted clergy, who might rob us of the means of knowledge and then inculcate on credulous minds what ſentiments they pleaſe. Not a ſingle office or emolument in America is held by

preſcription.

prescription or hereditary right; but all at the dipofal of the people, and not a man on the continent, but drones and villains, who has not the privilege of frequently choosing his legislators and impeaching his magistrates for mal-administration. Such principles form the basis of our American governments; the first and only governments on earth that are founded on the true principles of equal liberty and properly guarded from corruption.

The legislatures of the American states are the only legislatures on earth, which are *wholly* dependent on the people at large; and Congress is as dependent on the several states, as the legislatures are on their constituents. The members of Congress are chosen by the legislatures*, removable by them at pleasure, dependant on them for subsistence and responsible to their constituents for their conduct. But this is not all. After having been delegated three years, the confederation renders them ineligible for the term of three years more; when they must return, mingle with the people and become private citizens. At the same time, their interest is the same with that of the people; for enjoying no exclusive privileges but what are temporary, they cannot knowingly enact oppressive laws, because they involve themselves, their families and estates in all the mischiefs that result from such laws.

People therefore who attempt to terrify us with apprehensions of losing our liberties, because other states have lost theirs, betray an ignorance of history and of the principles of our confederation. I will not undertake to say that the government of the American states will not be corrupted or degenerate into tyranny. But I venture to assert, that if it should, it will be the fault of the people. If the people continue to choose their representatives annually and the choice of delegates to Congress should remain upon it's present footing, that body can never become

* In eleven states. In the other two, they are elected by the people. This is a defect, however, in the constitutions of those states, as the delegates, when chosen by the people, are immediately removable by the assembly and their place may be supplied without a reason given. The privilege of the people therefore nothing.

become tyrants. A meaſure partially oppreſſive may be reſolved upon, but while the principles of repreſentation, which are always in the power of the people, remain uncorrupted, ſuch a meaſure can be of no long continuance. The beſt conſtitution of government may degenerate from its purity, through a variety of cauſes; but the confederation of theſe ſtates is better ſecured than any government on earth, and leſs liable to corruption from any quarter.

There is the ſame danger that the conſtitutions of the ſeveral ſtates will become tyrannical, as that the principles of federal government will be corrupted. The ſtates in their collective capacity have no more reaſon to dread an uncontrolable power in Congreſs, than they have in their individual capacity, to dread the uncontrolable power of their own legiſlatures. Their ſecurity in both inſtances is, an equal repreſentation, the dependence, the reſponſibility and the rotation of their repreſentatives. Theſe articles conſtitute the baſis of our liberties, and will be an effectual ſecurity, ſo long as the people are wiſe enough to maintain the principles of the confederation.

I beg leavehere to obſerve that a ſtate was never yet deſtroyed by a corrupt or a wicked adminiſtration. Weakneſs and wickedneſs, in the executive department, may produce innumerable evils; but ſo long as the principles of a conſtitution remain uncorrupted, their vigour will always reſtore good order. Every ſtride of tyranny in the beſt governments in Europe, has been effected by breaking over ſome conſtitutional barriers. But where a conſtitution is formed by the people and unchangable but by their authority, the progreſs of corruption muſt be extremely ſlow, and perhaps tyranny can never be eſtabliſhed in ſuch government, except upon a general habit of indolence and vice.

What do the ſtates obtain by reſerving to themſelves the right of deciding on the propriety of the reſolutions of Congreſs? The great advantage of having every meaſure defeated, our frontiers expoſed to ſavages, the debts of the ſtates unpaid and accumulating, national faith violated, commerce reſtricted and inſulted, one ſtate filching ſome intereſt from another, and the whole body, linked together by cobwebs and ſhadows, the jeſt and the ridicule of the world. This is not a chimerical deſcription; it is a literal repreſentation of facts as they now exiſt. One ſtate found it could make ſome advantages by refuſing the impoſt. Congreſs have reaſoned with their legiſlature, and by incontrovertible proofs have pointed out the impropriety of the refuſal, but all to no purpoſe. Thus one fiftieth part of the ſtates counteracts a meaſure that the other ſtates ſuppoſe not only beneficial, but neceſſary; a meaſure, on which the diſcharge of our public debt and our national faith, moſt obviouſly depend. Can a government, thus feeble and disjointed, anſwer any valuable purpoſe? Can commutative juſtice between the ſtates ever be obtained? Can public debts be diſcharged and credit ſupported? Can America ever be reſpected by her enemies, when one of her own ſtates can, year after year, abuſe her weakneſs with impunity? No, the American ſtates, ſo celebrated for their wiſdom and valour in the late ſtruggle for freedom and empire, will be the contempt of nations, unleſs they can unite their force and carry into effect all the conſtitutional meaſures of Congreſs, whether thoſe meaſures reſpect themſelves or foreign nations.

The articles of confederation ordain, that the public expences ſhall be defrayed out of a common treaſury. But where is this treaſury? Congreſs preſcribe a meaſure for ſupplying this treaſury; but the ſtates do not approve of the meaſure; each ſtate will take its own way and its own time, and perhaps not ſupply its contingent of money at all. Is this an adherence to the articles of our union? It certainly is not; and the ſtates that refuſe a compliance with the general meaſures of the continent, would, under a good government, be conſidered as rebels. Such a conduct amounts to treaſon, for it ſtrikes at the foundation of government.

Permit me to aſk every candid American, how ſociety could

could exist, if every man assumed the right of sacrificing his neighbours property to his own interest? Are there no rights to be relinquished, no sacrifices to be made for the sake of enjoying the benefits of civil government? If every town in Rhode-Island, even the smallest, could annihilate every act of the legislature, could that state exist? Were such a selfish system to prevail generally, there would be an end of government and civil society would become a curse. A social state would be less eligible than a savage state, in proportion as knowledge would be increased and knaves multiplied. Local inconveniences and local interests never ought to disappoint a measure of general utility. If there is not power enough in government to remedy these evils, by obliging private interests to give way to public, discord will pervade the state, and terminate in a revolution. Such a power must exist some where, and if people will quarrel with good government, there are innumerable opportunities for some daring ambitious genius to erect a monarchy on civil dissensions. In America, there is no danger of an aristocracy; but the transition from popular anarchy to monarchy, is very natural and often very easy. If these states have any change of government to fear, it is a monarchy. Nothing but the creation of a sovereign power over the whole, with authority to compel obedience to legal measures, can ever prevent a revolution in favour of one monarchy or more. This event may be distant, but is not the less certain. America has it now in her power to create a supreme power over the whole continent, sufficient to answer all the ends of government, without abridging the rights or destroying the sovereignty of a single state. But should the extreme jealousy of the states, prevent the lodgment of such a power in a body of men chosen by themselves and removable at pleasure, such a power will inevitably create itself in the course of events.

The confederation has sketched out a most excellent form of continental government. The ninth article recites the powers of Congress, which are perhaps nearly sufficient to answer the ends of our union, were there any method of enforcing

their

their refolutions. It is there faid what powers fhall be exercifed by Congrefs; but no penalty is annexed to difobedience. What purpofe would the laws of a ftate anfwer, if they might be evaded with impunity? and if there were no penalty annexed to a breach of them? A law without a penalty is mere *advice*; a magiftrate, without the power of punifhing, is a *cypher*. Here is the *great defect* in the articles of our federal government. Unlefs Congrefs can be vefted with the fame authority to compel obedience to their refolutions, that a legiflature in any ftate has to enforce obedience to the laws of that ftate, the exiftence of fuch a body is entirely needlefs and will not be of long duration. I repeat what I have before faid. The idea of governing thirteen ftates and uniting their interefts by mere *refolves* and *recommendations*, without any penalty annexed to a non-compliance, is a ridiculous farce, a burlefque on government, and a reproach to America.

Let Congrefs be empowered to call forth the force of the continent, if neceffary, to carry into effect thofe meafures which they have a right to frame. Let the prefident, be, *ex officio*, fupreme magiftrate, cloathed with authority to execute the laws of Congrefs, in the fame manner as the governors of the ftates, are to execute the laws of the ftates. Let the fuperintendant of finance have the power of receiving the public monies and iffuing warrants for collection, in the manner the treafurer has, in Connecticut. Let every executive officer have power to enforce the laws, which fall within his province. At the fame time, let them be accountable for their adminiftration. Let penalties be annexed to every fpecies of male-adminiftration and exacted with fuch rigour as is due to juftice and the public fafety. In fhort, let the whole fyftem of legiflation, be the peculiar right of the delegates in Congrefs, who are always under the control of the people; and let the whole adminiftration be vefted in magiftrates as few as poffible in number, and fubject to the control of Congrefs only. Let every precaution be ufed in *framing* laws, but let no part of the fubjects be able to refift the execution. Let the people keep, and *forever keep*, the fole right of legiflation in their own reprefentatives; but diveft themfelves wholly of any right to the adminiftration. Let every ftate referve its fovereign right of directing its own internal affairs; but give to Congrefs the fole right of conducting the general affairs of the continent. Such a plan of government is practicable; and I believe, the only plan that will preferve the faith, the dignity and the union of thefe American ftates.

I fhall juft hint feveral other matters, that may ferve, in a more remote manner, to confirm the union of thefe ftates.

Education or a general diffufion of knowledge among all claffes of men, is an article that deferves peculiar attention. Science liberalizes men and removes the moft inveterate prejudices. Every prejudice, every diffocial paffion is an enemy to a friendly intercourfe and the fuel of difcord. Nothing can be more illiber-

al

al than the prejudices of the ſouthern ſtates againſt New-England manners. They deride our manners and by that deriſion betray the want of manners themſelves. However different may be the cuſtoms and faſhions of different ſtates, yet thoſe of the ſouthern are as ridiculous as thoſe of the northern. The fact is, neither one nor the other are the ſubjects of ridicule and contempt. Particular diſtricts have local peculiarities; but cuſtom gives all an equal degree of propriety. It is remarked of the Greeks as a great indelicacy of manners, that they held all the world, except themſelves, to be barbarians. The people of Congo think the world to be the work of angels; except their own country, which they hold to be the work of the ſupreme architect. The Greenlanders make a mock of Europeans or Kablunets, as they call them. They deſpiſe arts and ſciences and value themſelves on their ſkill in catching ſeals, which they conceive to be the only uſeful art*. Juſt as abſurd as theſe, are the prejudices between the ſtates. Education will gradually eradicate them, and a growing intercourſe will harmonize the feelings and the views of all the citizens.

Next to the removal of local prejudices, the annihilation of local intereſts between the ſtates deſerves their conſideration. Each ſtate wiſhes to enrich itſelf as much as poſſible; but it never ought to be done at the expence of a neighbour. All impoſts and duties upon goods purchaſed of one ſtate by another or carried in a port of another ſtate either by neceſſity or accident, are the effect of narrow views, and of ſelfiſh, unſociable, ungenerous principles, that degrade any ſtate where they operate. The ſtates may lay what dutes they pleaſe upon foreigners—this is no more than honeſt—but they ought to conſider their ſeveral intereſts as one—they ought to encourage the commerce of each other—they ought to promote ſuch an intercourſe as will conciliate rather than alienate each others affections. Every injury done by any particular ſtate to the union, will ultimately recoil upon itſelf with accumulated weight. It is the act of a madman to ſacrifice the happineſs of his life to a moment's pleaſure; and none but a fool would pull the houſe about his ears to find a ſhilling. So long as the ſtates are making every advantage out of each other, racking invention to enlarge their own bounds, and augment their wealth and reſpectability at each other's expence, jealouſy, ill-will and reproaches will diſturb the harmony of public meaſures and contibute to the diſſolution of all continental connections. Not only ſhould the ſtates avoid wringing property from each other by duties on articles of commerce; but alſo an extention of territory in ſuch a manner as to create reciprocal jealouſies. All the ſuperior reſpectability that a ſingle ſtate gains above others

* A faſhionable buck in Carolina deſpiſes literature. A man of ſcience, without the addreſs of the *beau monde*, is ridiculed and placed almoſt among the ſervants. In the ſouthern ſtates, gaming, fox hunting and horſe-racing are the height of ambition; induſtry is reſerved for ſlaves. In the northern ſtates, induſtry and the cultivation of the arts and ſciences, diſtinguiſh the people. Which diſcover the beſt taſte?

others by its extent and wealth, detracts so much from the strength and harmony of the union. In order to have our union complete and permanent, all the states should have an equal influence in public deliberations. The want of such equality is a capital misfortune—it had well nigh prevented our confederation—and has produced other sensible inconveniences.

The abolition of slavery is a matter intimately connected with the policy of these states. The northern states would hardly feel such an event—the southern would at present suffer by it most sensibly. But slavery ought to be viewed as to its present tendency and remote consequences. At present it is the bane of industry and virtue. The slaves in the southern states support luxury, vice and indolence more than all other causes. They may enrich their owners; but render them too often useless members of society. Nor are slaves so profitable as white people; for one man, who lives by his industry, and eats hearty food, will do as much labour as five negroes. Were the plantations leased for small rents or the fee of the soil vested in men, who have the prospect of gain by their labour, they would be better cultivated and yield more produce to the owners. But aside of the detestable principle of subjecting one man to the service of another, which dishonours a free government, and the evil of supporting luxury the bane of society, slavery inspires other principles repugnant to the genius of our American constitutions. It cherishes a spirit of supercilious contempt—a haughty, unsocial, aristocratic temper, inconsistent with that equality which is the basis of our governments and the happiness of human society.

An uniformity in the general principles of each constitution, deserves attention. Some defects may be found in all: I will mention but one, which is not common to all; the exclusion of clergymen from all civil offices. Considering the evils that mankind have suffered from Eclesiastics in Europe, it is no wonder that Americans should dread their power. But men, in avoiding one error, run into another. We are not apt to attend to the difference of circumstances. The clergy in America do not and ought not, as a body, to form a part of government. But why, as individuals, they should be excluded from all the emoluments of government, and all share of making the laws to which they are subject, is to me inconceiveable. Merchants, mechanics and farmers as distinct bodies, have no power, but as individuals, they are elegible to offices of trust and profit, and so ought to be eclesiastics. Here is the distinction and the reasoning applies with equal force, to every profession.

Must clergymen, because they are employed about spiritual concerns, be deprived of the privileges of society? But aside of the flagrant injustice of such exclusion, the measure counteracts its own end. When ecclesiastics, as a body, are admitted to a share of legislation, they may form combinations dangerous to a state. To prevent this danger, some states exclude them totally from

from civil offices and thus make them foes to the government by a most tyrannical distinction. Such an exclusion therefore produces the very effect, which it was intended to prevent. The state of New-York is a witness of this truth. Add to this the inevitable tendency of such an exclusion to discourage men of knowledge and liberality from entering into a most useful and necessary profession. Surely no state ought to interweave, into its constitution, a general discouragement of a profession, calculated at least to promote the peace and happiness of society. Should I be asked what privileges clergymen ought to enjoy? I would answer, the same as other citizens. This would annihilate their power as a body, by scattering its force, by leveling a distinction of orders, and blending the civil and ecclesiastical interests in one *indivisible interest*.

The same principle, which excludes clergymen from civil offices, and which has introduced test laws and subscription of creeds, into some of the American constitutions, would have justified the religious wars in France and Germany; nay, the same principle would have justified Nero and Dioclesian in extirpating christianity and committing the bible to the flames. The principle would only be extended further in one case than in the other. If there is in the system of things, such a thing as true religion, and a spirit of pure benevolence; religious establishments, sacramental tests, articles of faith, partial exclusion from emoluments, and that illiberal pride which sanctifies our own opinions and damns all others, will forever banish them from human society. Had it not been for these barriers, invented to guard human absurdities, millions of lives would have been saved, and the members of every enlightened community would have been of *one religion*.

America is an independent empire, and ought to assume a national character. Nothing can be more ridiculous, than a servile imitation of the manners, the language, and the vices of foreigners. For setting aside the infancy of our government and our inability to support the fashionable amusements of Europe, nothing can betray a more despicable disposition in Americans, than to be the apes of Europeans. An American ought not to ask what is the custom of London and Paris; but what is proper for us in our circumstances and what is becoming our dignity? Instead of this, what is the fact? Why every fashionable folly is brought from Europe and adopted without scruple in our dress, our manners and our conversation. All our ladies, even those of the most scanty fortune, must dress like a dutchess in London; every shop-keeper must be as great a rake as an English lord; while the *belles* and the *beaux*, with tastes too refined for a vulgar language, must, in all their discourse, mingle a spice of *sans souci* and *je ne scai quoi*.

But there is no reasoning with custom nor with fashion. We shall probably learn the arts and virtues of Europeans; but certainly,

tainly, their vices and follies. In politics, our weakness will render us the dupes of their power and artifice; in manners, we shall be the slaves of their barbers and their coxcombs.

But however important may be the remote consequences of a corruption of manners; yet much nearer concerns now demand our attention. Our union is so feeble, that no provision is made for discharging our debts. France calls for interest and that seriously. Our credit, our faith solemnly pledged, is at stake. Unless we constitute a power at the head of the states, sufficient to compel them to act in concert, I now predict not only a dissolution of our federal connection, but a rupture with our national creditors. A war in Europe may possibly suspend this event; but it must certainly take place, unless we sacrifice our jealousy to our true interest.

Three things demand our early and careful attention; a general diffusion of knowledge; the encouragement of industry, frugality and virtue; and a sovereign power at the head of the states. *All* are essential to our peace and prosperity; but on an energetic continental government principally depend our tranquility at home and our respectability among foreign nations.

We ought to generalize our ideas and our measures. We ought not to consider ourselves as inhabitants of a particular state only; but as *Americans;* as the common subjects of a great empire. We cannot and ought not wholly to divest ourselves of provincial views and attachments; but we should subordinate them to the general interests of the continent. As a member of a family, every individual has some domestic interests; as a member of a corporation, he has other interests; as an inhabitant of a state, he has a more extensive interest; as a citizen and subject of the American empire, he has a national interest far superior to all others. Every relation in society constitutes some obligations, which are proportional to the magnitude of the society. A good prince does not ask what will be for the interest of a county or small district in his dominions; but what will promote the prosperity of his kingdom? In the same manner, the citizens of this new world, should enquire, not what will aggrandize this town or this state; but what will augment the power, secure the tranquility, multiply the subjects, and advance the opulence, the dignity and the virtues of the United States. Self interest, both in morals and politics, is and ought to be the ruling principle of mankind; but this principle must operate in perfect conformity to social and political obligations. Narrow views and illiberal prejudices may for a time produce a selfish system of politics in each state; but a few years experience will correct our ideas of self-interest, and convince us that a selfishness which excludes others from a participation of benefits, is, in all cases, self-ruin, and that *provincial interest* is inseperable from *national interest.*

THE END.

www.ingramcontent.com/pod-product-compliance
Lightning Source LLC
LaVergne TN
LVHW091636100826
845152LV00002B/54

* 9 7 8 1 5 8 4 7 7 8 5 6 1 *